TOP **10**
MOSCOW

MATT WILLIS

EYEWITNESS TRAVEL

Left **New Ballet performance** Center **Arbatskaya metro station** Right **Kuskovo Estate**

LONDON, NEW YORK,
MELBOURNE, MUNICH AND DELHI
www.dk.com

Design, Editorial, and Picture Research by
Quadrum Solutions, Krishnamai, 33B, Sir
Pochkanwala Road, Worli, Mumbai, India

Reproduced by Colourscan, Singapore
Printed and bound in China by
Leo Paper Products Ltd

First American Edition, 2010
10 11 12 13 10 9 8 7 6 5 4 3 2 1

Published in the United States by
DK Publishing, 375 Hudson Street,
New York, New York 10014

**Copyright 2010 © Dorling Kindersley Limited,
London, A Penguin Company**

Published in Great Britain by Dorling Kindersley
Limited.

ISSN 1479-344X

ISBN 978 0 7566 5723 9

Within each Top 10 list in this book, no hierarchy
of quality or popularity is implied. All 10 are, in
the editor's opinion, of roughly equal merit..

We're trying to be cleaner and greener:

- we recycle waste and switch things off
- we use paper from responsibly managed
  forests whenever possible
- we ask our printers to actively reduce
  water and energy consumption
- we check out our suppliers' working
  conditions – they never use child labour

**Find out more about our values and
best practices at www.dk.com**

Contents

Moscow's Top 10

The information in this DK Eyewitness Top 10 Travel Guide is checked regularly.
Every effort has been made to ensure that this book is as up-to-date as possible at the time of
going to press. Some details, however, such as telephone numbers, opening hours, prices,
gallery hanging arrangements and travel information are liable to change. The publishers
cannot accept responsibility for any consequences arising from the use of this book, nor for
any material on third party websites, and cannot guarantee that any website address in this
book will be a suitable source of travel information. We value the views and suggestions of
our readers very highly. Please write to: Publisher, DK Eyewitness Travel Guides,
Dorling Kindersley, 80 Strand, London WC2R 0RL.

Cover: Front – **4Corners Images:** Marcello Bertinetti main; **DK Images:** Demetrio Carrasco bl. Spine – **DK Images:**
Demetrio Carrasco b. Back – **Alamy Images:** Yadid Levy tr; **DK Images:** Demetrio Carrasco tc, tl.

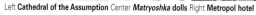

Left **Cathedral of the Assumption** Center *Matryoshka* dolls Right **Metropol hotel**

Left **Historical Museum, Red Square** Right **Alexander Gardens**

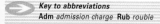

Key to abbreviations
Adm *admission charge* **Rub** *rouble*

3

MOSCOW'S
TOP 10

MOSCOW'S TOP 10

🔟 Moscow's Highlights

Despite Stalin's destruction of much of Moscow's architectural heritage, what remains is enough to convey the impression of a medieval capital that collided with a Soviet juggernaut. It is a city where petite onion-domed churches and 19th-century mansions compete with epic neo-Gothic skyscrapers and ten-lane ring roads. Ironically, Communism's greatest contribution to the city – the magnificent metro system – lies deep underground. In recent years bold modern structures have been added to Moscow's progressive skyline and Muscovites have begun to recover pride in their city by funding the restoration of lost landmarks such as the Cathedral of Christ the Saviour (see p74).

St Basil's Cathedral
Built in the 16th century, during the uncertain times of Ivan the Terrible, Moscow's magnificent centrepiece continues to be as enthralling as ever *(see pp8–9)*.

Red Square
The historic square, also called Krasnaya Ploshchad, is home to two of Moscow's most famous sights – St Basil's Cathedral and the Lenin Mausoleum *(see pp10–11)*.

Arbatskaya

Cathedral of the Assumption
The cathedral's stunning gilt frescoed interior has hosted coronation ceremonies since the 16th century *(see pp12–13)*.

State Armoury
With its array of gleaming weaponry and priceless treasures, including exquisite diamonds and Fabergé eggs, the Armoury offers a fascinating insight into the life of Russia's nobility *(see pp14–15)*.

Pushkin Museum of Fine Arts
This superb collection takes in some 500,000 masterly artworks from across the globe, including ancient artifacts, sculptures and paintings *(see pp16–17)*.

Bolshoy Theatre
Home to one of the oldest ballet companies in the world, the Bolshoy is Europe's second-largest opera house, after Milan's La Scala. Performances are currently being staged at an alternative venue while the grand auditorium undergoes renovations *(see pp18–19)*.

Tretyakov Gallery
From its humble beginnings in the family home of the art enthusiast Pavel Tretyakov, this gallery has evolved into one of the world's greatest collections of Russian art *(see pp20–23)*.

Metro Stations
Moscow's palatial metro stations are artistic monuments in their own right. Each station offers a different depiction of the Soviet ideal; some are filled with striking sculptures, while others feature mosaics or stained-glass panels *(see pp24–5)*.

Novodevichiy Convent
This UNESCO-listed convent is a wonderfully preserved example of 17th-century Moscow Baroque architecture; it also boasts the city's most famous graveyard *(see pp26–7)*.

Kolomenskoe Estate
A favourite summer home of the tsars, Kolomenskoe enjoys an idyllic location beside the Moskva river and makes for a lovely day out *(see pp28–9)*.

St Basil's Cathedral

With red-brick towers and swirling onion domes, this gloriously colourful cathedral is perhaps Russia's most emblematic building. Ivan the Terrible ordered its construction to celebrate capturing the Tatar stronghold of Kazan, 800 km (500 miles) east of Moscow, in 1552. The cathedral was designed with eight chapels, each representing a successful assault made on Kazan. A ninth chapel was added later to cover the grave of Basil the Blessed, the pious ascetic to whom the cathedral owes its popular name.

Visitors inside St Basil's Cathedral

🎵 Linger in the Central Chapel where you might hear the cathedral's male choir sing promotional excerpts from their CD of Orthodox chants.

🍴 The nearby GUM shopping mall *(see p64)* has plenty of cafés and ice-cream parlours.

• Map N3
• Krasnaya Ploshchad 2
• Metro: Okhotnyy Ryad, Ploshchad Revolyutsii
• Open May–Nov: 11am–6pm; Dec–Apr: 11am–5pm
• Adm: 150 Rub

Top 10 Features

1. Tiled Gallery
2. Iconostases
3. Tent-Roofed Bell Tower
4. Internal Wooden Staircase
5. Onion Domes
6. St Basil's Chapel
7. Chapel of St Cyprian
8. Interior Frescoes
9. St Basil's Name
10. History Exhibition

1 Tiled Gallery

The warren of narrow galleries *(above)* and stairways connecting St Basil's chapels over different levels was covered over in the 17th century and subsequently decorated with elaborate tiles featuring floral and geometric designs.

2 Iconostases

The cathedral's nine iconostases *(right)*, symbolizing the separation between the divine and the earthly world, comprise over 400 icons from the Moscow and Novgorod schools of icon painting.

3 Tent-Roofed Bell Tower

Added to St Basil's Cathedral during the late 17th century, the bell tower *(left)* is located at the south-east corner. It rang until 1918, when the Communist authorities closed the cathedral and melted down its bells. It was not until 1997 that new bells were cast and once again rang out over Moscow.

4 Internal Wooden Staircase

Leading up to the Chapel of the Intercession, this spiral wooden staircase *(below)* remained hidden for hundreds of years until its accidental discovery in the 1970s during renovation work. It is now open to the public.

5 Onion Domes

The cathedral's central tower is surrounded by onion domes: four large and four small *(centre)*. Originally gilded, they received their first full-colour treatment in 1670.

6 St Basil's Chapel

In 1588, Tsar Fyodor commissioned a ninth chapel, with a small dome, to contain the relics of Basil the Blessed (1468–1552).

7 Chapel of St Cyprian

Each of the original eight chapels honours the saint upon whose feast day an assault on Kazan occured. St Cyprian's Day was that of the penultimate attack on the stronghold. With a striped blue-and-white dome, this chapel is one of the cathedral's largest.

8 Interior Frescoes

The interior of each chapel is illuminated by 19th-century oil paintings and the bright colours of freshly restored frescoes *(above)* dating back to the 16th century.

9 St Basil's Name

The cathedral only adopted its popular moniker after St Basil was interred here. It was originally named the Cathedral of the Intercession of the Virgin on the Moat.

10 History Exhibition

A small exhibition inside the main entrance chronicles St Basil's history and includes a display of 16th-century weaponry used during Ivan the Terrible's campaign against Kazan.

Lucky Escapes

St Basil's Cathedral has twice escaped destruction. During his conquest of Moscow in 1812 Napoleon ordered its demolition, but the task was abandoned when rain dampened the gunpowder. Stalin contemplated knocking it down to facilitate the exit of troops parading across Red Square, but was stopped by the architect Baranovsky, who threatened to cut his own throat. The gesture earned Baranovsky five years of hard labour.

For information on Moscow's history See pp32–3.

Red Square

Red Square (Krasnaya Ploshchad) has been at the heart of Moscow for over 500 turbulent years, and its grand buildings recall the city's eventful history. Here, Ivan the Terrible mutilated prisoners before repenting of his sins at Lobnoe Mesto; it was he who funded the construction of St Basil's Cathedral. In 1812 a victorious Napoleon addressed his troops on the square, while stabling their horses in the cathedral. Lenin Mausoleum was added by the Communists, who later demolished both the Resurrection Gate and Kazan Cathedral to make way for enormous military parades. The square has been restored to its pre-Soviet appearance.

St Basil's Cathedral
Moscow's enduring highlight, with its eclectic mix of colourful domes *(above)* and lovely chapel interiors, has stood here since 1561 *(see pp8–9)*.

Kilometre Zero, near Resurrection Gate

🕐 Before queuing for the Lenin Mausoleum, leave large bags and any photographic equipment at the Historical Museum's cloakroom to avoid being refused entry.

🍴 Facing Red Square, the Bosco Café *(see p67)* in the GUM shopping mall has a great range of ice creams and desserts.

• Map M3
• Krasnaya Ploshchad
• Metro: Ploshchad Revolyutsii, Teatralnaya, Okhotnyy Ryad

Top 10 Features
1. Statue of Marshal Zhukov
2. St Basil's Cathedral
3. Lobnoe Mesto
4. Statue of Minin and Pozharskiy
5. GUM
6. Kilometre Zero
7. Resurrection Gate
8. Lenin Mausoleum
9. Historical Museum
10. Kazan Cathedral

Statue of Marshal Zhukov
Astride a stallion, Marshal Zhukov *(below)* raises his palm in symbolic defence of the Kremlin. In 1944 he successfully lifted the siege of Leningrad, before pushing back the Germans and capturing Berlin in 1945.

Lobnoe Mesto
Despite its ominous name, meaning "execution place", this has only ever been used as a speaker's platform; leaders have made proclamations from here since the 16th century.

Statue of Minin and Pozharskiy
This dramatic statue depicts the two legendary Russian heroes who drove Polish troops out of the Kremlin in 1612.

GUM

5 Occupying the eastern side of the square, this glitzy 19th-century shopping mall *(below)* was once the largest of its kind in Europe. Three gleaming arcades are connected by elegant walkways *(see p64)*.

Kilometre Zero

6 The brass plaque in the ground here marks the point from which all distances from Moscow are measured. The spot is scattered with coins for luck.

Resurrection Gate

7 Built in 1995, this is a copy of the original 17th-century gate demolished by Stalin to allow parading troops easier access to the square.

Lenin Mausoleum

8 Designed by Aleksey Shchusev, the mausoleum features a rooftop terrace from which leaders might view military parades *(see p63)*.

Kremlin Wall Graves

These graves *(see p63)* have been used to inter the ashes of Soviet heroes since 1917, when 200 revolutionaries were buried here. Soviet leaders were buried in individual tombs. Stalin's body was embalmed and laid beside that of Lenin, where it remained until 1961, when it was removed and buried following Khrushchev's de-Stalinization programme.

Historical Museum

9 This imposing red-brick building *(centre)* houses a fascinating array of over 20,000 exhibits, including Palaeolithic mammoth remains *(see p63)*.

Kazan Cathedral

10 Rebuilt in 1993 in the style of the 17th-century original, this exquisite cathedral *(right)* houses a replica of the miracle-working Icon of the Kazan Virgin *(see p37)*.

Between the arches of the Resurrection Gate lies the tiny Iverskaya Chapel, where tsars would pray before entering the Kremlin.

▣10 Cathedral of the Assumption

Originally founded in 1326, the cathedral was redesigned in 1470 by Italian architect Aristotle Fioravanti in Renaissance spirit. For centuries it hosted Russia's most important ceremonies, including the coronation of Ivan the Terrible in 1547 and the inaugurations and burials of the patriarchs and metropolitans of the Orthodox Church. The cathedral retained its importance even after the capital was moved to St Petersburg in 1713, but was closed by the Communists in 1918; religious services resumed in 1990.

Graceful 15th-century south portal

🜊 The best views of the Kremlin's cathedral towers are from the south, from the opposite bank of the Moskva river.

☕ There are no cafés within the Kremlin; the nearest are those at Manezh Mall *(see p52)*.

- Map M4
- Kremlin
- Metro: Aleksandrovskiy sad, Biblioteka im. Lenina, Borovitskaya
- (495) 697 0349 (Call in advance to book a guided tour)
- Open 10am–5pm Fri–Wed
- Adm: 350 Rub
- www.kreml.ru

Top 10 Features

1. Patriarch's Seat
2. Iconostasis
3. Tabernacle
4. Frescoes
5. St George Icon
6. Miraculous Virgin of Vladimir Icon
7. Monomakh Throne
8. Tomb of Metropolitan St Peter
9. Tomb of Metropolitan St Iona
10. Harvest Chandelier

▣ Patriarch's Seat

This white-stone prayer seat was used by metropolitans and patriarchs from the 16th century. It was from this chair that Metropolitan St Philip II (1507–69) refused to bless Ivan the Terrible in 1568.

▣ Iconostasis

The gleaming iconostasis *(right)*, which dominates the cathedral, was built in 1813. The original iconostasis, dating from 1652, was destroyed by Napoleonic troops the previous year. It comprises a remarkable series of gilt-framed icons rising five levels to a grand 14th-century portrait of Christ.

▣ Tabernacle

Cast in 1624, the latticed bronze tabernacle served as a repository for Russia's collection of holy relics, including one of the four nails used to crucify Christ. Today it contains the remains of Patriarch Germogen (1530–1612).

↪ *The patriarch heads the Russian Orthodox Church, while metropolitans (archbishops) are responsible for regions or cities.*

Frescoes 4

The frescoes adorning the interior were painted in 1511 and a gilt layer was added 150 years later. The four huge central pillars *(right)* depict portraits of 140 martyrs.

St George Icon 5

Encased by glass, this 12th-century icon depicting a youthful St George was discovered under a layer of paint on the reverse of another icon in 1930.

Miraculous Virgin of Vladimir Icon 6

The revered 16th-century copy of the Virgin of Vladimir icon *(below)* is kept in a small gilt tabernacle beside the iconostasis.

Monomakh Throne 7

Installed as Ivan the Terrible's prayer seat in 1551, this elaborately carved throne owes its name to scenes on its rear panel depicting the life of Prince Vladimir Monomakh (1053–1155).

Tomb of Metropolitan St Peter 8

St Peter founded the cathedral in 1326 and his tomb is contained within a shrine with silver pillars and a canopy topped with a gilt dome.

Tomb of Metropolitan St Iona 9

St Iona became Moscow's metropolitan in 1448. His gold and silver canopied shrine is one of the most sumptuous tombs in the cathedral.

Harvest Chandelier 10

This chandelier *(right)* was made from gold that Napoleon's soldiers looted during their occupation of Moscow in 1812, and later abandoned.

Unusual History

During Napoleon's occupation in 1812 the cathedral was one of many churches used to stable horses. To combat the cold, French troops cut up its 15th-century iconostasis to use as firewood. Stalin, who had a Christian upbringing, allegedly ordered a secret service to be held here in 1941 when the German army was approaching Moscow.

A vivid fresco portraying the Day of Judgement takes up much of the cathedral's western wall.

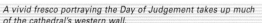

⟦TOP⟧10 State Armoury

The Kremlin's fabulous collection of weaponry and treasure offers a fascinating insight into the immense wealth and power enjoyed by the Russian aristocracy throughout the centuries. Moscow's Grand Princes began storing their valuables in the Kremlin's cellars as early as the 14th century, but when space ran short a stone treasury was built between the fortress's cathedrals. The collection was first put on public display in 1806 and the current State Armoury was purpose-built as a museum on the orders of Tsar Nicholas I. Designed by Konstantin Ton in 1844, the building was completed in 1851. Here you will find remarkable ceremonial carriages, priceless churchware, glittering thrones and some of the world's largest jewels, including the famous Orlov Diamond.

Elegant interior of the State Armoury

🎫 Tickets should be purchased in advance from the kiosk at Kutafya Tower.

Tickets for the Diamond Fund can only be purchased inside the Armoury.

Large bags must be deposited in the cloakroom beneath Kutafya Tower.

🍴 For refreshments, visit the nearby Manezh Mall *(see p52)*.

- Map M4
- Kremlin
- (495) 697 0349
- Metro: Biblioteka im. Lenina, Borovitskaya, Aleksandrovskiy sad
- Admittance at 10am, noon, 2:30pm, 4:30pm
- Adm: 350 Rub
- www.kreml.ru

Top 10 Features

1. Diamond Throne
2. Catherine the Great's Wedding Dress
3. Russian Weaponry
4. Ceremonial Saddlery and Carriages
5. Miniature Carriages
6. Crown of Monomakh
7. The Diamond Fund
8. The Orlov Diamond
9. Ambassadorial Gifts
10. Fabergé Eggs

1 Diamond Throne
This gem-encrusted sandalwood throne *(below)* was gifted to Tsar Alexius in the 17th century by Armenians hopeful of securing Russian trade rights.

2 Catherine the Great's Wedding Dress
Among the royal outfits on display is Catherine the Great's finely embroidered silver wedding dress. Her loveless marriage at 16 to Peter III led to his abdication and her assumption of power.

3 Russian Weaponry
The Round Hall has a fine array of 12th-century Russian weaponry. Ceremonial sabres and scabbards sit alongside 17th-century flintlock pistols and iron chainmail armour.

4 Ceremonial Saddlery and Carriages

The saddlery on display includes Ivan the Terrible's velvet-covered saddle and a harness given to Catherine the Great by Turkish Sultan Abdul Hamid. The oldest carriage here (left) was a gift to Boris I from King James I in 1604.

5 Miniature Carriages

Among the collection of royal carriages is a delightful pair of miniature carriages that were produced in the 17th century for Peter the Great's children.

6 Crown of Monomakh

Edged with sable fur and topped with jewels and a gold cross, this ancient crown was first used at Ivan the Terrible's coronation in 1547.

7 The Diamond Fund

Among the Fund's sparkling highlights are the Large Emperor's Crown (above), with 5,000 diamonds, and the Shah Diamond, presented to Tsar Nicholas I by Fath Ali Shah as compensation for the murder of Russia's ambassador in Persia.

8 The Orlov Diamond

The world's fourth-largest diamond adorns the Imperial Sceptre. Taken from an Indian temple, it was one of the many presents given to Catherine the Great by her lover, Count Grigoriy Orlov.

9 Ambassadorial Gifts

Lavish gifts received from diplomats and merchants include English Tudor silverware, a 140-piece Sèvres porcelain dessert service gifted to Emperor Alexander I by Napoleon in 1807, and a wonderful silver decanter given to Tsar Alexius in 1665.

10 Fabergé Eggs

The Armoury owns one of the world's largest collections of Fabergé eggs (left), produced as Easter gifts for Tsar Nicholas II and his family between 1885 and 1917. Among them is an exquisite example containing a tiny model of the Tsar's yacht.

Fabergé Fascination

The wealthy art collector Malcolm Forbes (1919–90) is credited with reviving the world's interest in Fabergé eggs. Between 1960 and 1990 he tracked down nine of the Russian royal family's eggs and paid large sums for them. His collection was put up for auction after his death in 1990 and was purchased by Russian oligarch Viktor Vekselberg.

The Diamond Fund features the world's biggest gold nugget, weighing 36.2 kg (80 lb).

Pushkin Museum of Fine Arts

This stately museum has amassed over 500,000 artworks since its inauguration in 1912. It was envisaged as an educational institution, and was initially filled with plaster casts of sculptural masterpieces along with a world-class selection of Egyptian relics. Subsequent political events led to the expansion of the collection far beyond its original parameters. The Communist policy of nationalizing private property brought many new artworks to the museum; it was further boosted when the government transferred thousands of pieces to it from St Petersburg's Hermitage. The museum's excellent collection of Impressionist, Post-Impressionist and Modernist art is housed next door in a new Gallery of European and American Art of the 19th–20th Century.

Exhibits in the Pushkin Museum of Fine Arts

⚙ Three neighbouring buildings house the majority of the museum's collection. A single ticket covering all the sites can be bought from the central museum building.

⚙ The museum's basement café serves reasonably priced snacks and cakes.

- Map L4
- Ulitsa Volkhonka 12
- (495) 697 9578
- Metro: Kropotkinskaya
- Open 10am–7pm Tue–Sun (10am–9pm Thu)
- Adm: 500 Rub
- www.museum.ru/gmii

Top 10 Features

1. Masterpieces in Plaster
2. Hay Wagon
3. Fayoum Portraits
4. Blue Dancers
5. Troy Treasure
6. Virgin and Child
7. Matisse and Picasso Collections
8. Bacchanalia
9. Rodchenko Collection
10. Monet Collection

1 Masterpieces in Plaster

Several rooms of the museum are filled with plaster casts of classic Greek and Roman sculptures *(centre)* and copies of works by Michelangelo and other Renaissance figures. These were originally intended as models for art students.

2 Hay Wagon

Jean-Baptiste-Camille Corot claimed that the desire to create landscapes outweighed everything else in his life. Painted in 1860, *Hay Wagon* captures his style as it moves towards Impressionism; light brush-strokes depict the freshness of the rural scene.

3 Fayoum Portraits

Found in the 1870s attached to mummies in the Fayoum region of Egypt, these remarkable portraits *(left)* demonstrate an extraordinary degree of realism. They were produced as death masks around the 1st century AD and form part of the museum's substantial Egyptian collection.

5 Troy Treasure

Also called Priam's Treasure, this 4,500-year-old collection of gold and silver dishes, goblets and jewellery was found in the lost city of Troy by German archaeologist Heinrich Schliemann in 1873.

4 Blue Dancers

Edgar Degas' outstanding 1898 pastel sketch *(above)*, showing the same dancer in multiple poses, illustrates the "random glance" method with which the artist conveyed fleeting impressions of a scene.

6 Virgin and Child

Despite its missing right-hand panel, this 16th-century work *(below)* by Lucas Cranach the Elder clearly displays the artist's skills as a leading figure of the German Renaissance. Its highlights are realism, use of perspective and the subtle inclusion of a cross above the child's head.

7 Matisse and Picasso Collections

In 1948 the gallery acquired works by Henri Matisse and Pablo Picasso from industrialist Sergey Shchukin. Among the prize exhibits are Matisse's *Spanish Woman with a Tambourine* (1909) and Picasso's *Young Acrobat on a Ball* (1905).

8 Bacchanalia

This masterpiece by Peter Paul Rubens is a fine example of 17th-century Baroque painting. It skilfully combines stark contrasts between dark and light with intense realism to hint at the inner passions of the subjects.

9 Rodchenko Collection

Hundreds of minimalist paintings and experimental photographs by Aleksandr Rodchenko (1891–1956) are on display alongside works by his wife Varvara Stepanova (1894–1958).

Looted German Treasure

In 1880 Heinrich Schliemann donated the Fayoum Treasure to Berlin's Imperial Museum. It remained there until 1945, when it disappeared after the city fell to the Red Army. Nothing more was heard about it until it went on display at the Pushkin Museum of Fine Arts in 1993. The treasure remains there despite an official agreement to return it to Germany.

10 Monet Collection

Originally part of Sergey Shchukin's private collection, the paintings by Claude Monet span over 30 years and chart the artist's development from the figurative *Luncheon on the Grass* (1866) to the Impressionistic *Rouen Cathedral* (1893).

 Peter Paul Rubens's Bacchanalia *hangs alongside a broad range of Flemish art from the same period.*

Bolshoy Theatre

Established in 1776, the Bolshoy theatre and ballet companies are among the oldest in the world. They were based in Moscow's Petrovsky Theatre until 1812, when the building was consumed by fire during Napoleon's invasion. In 1825 the Bolshoy Theatre, designed by Osip Bove (1784–1834), opened to instant international acclaim, but in 1853 it too was claimed by fire. Its restoration was overseen by architect Albert Kavos, who increased the building's height and chose the current decor. Today the Bolshoy retains its status as a world-class ballet and opera venue. The theatre is currently closed for renovation, but performances continue to be staged in the neighbouring New Bolshoy Theatre.

Scene from a historic performance

🕐 The Bolshoy has an online booking service and tickets can also be reserved by phone in English.

🍷 The theatre bar serves refreshments during intervals.

- Map M2
- Teatralnaya Ploshchad 1
- (495) 692 0818
- Metro: Teatralnaya
- Open 11am–7pm (ticket office)
- Adm: varies from 600 to 4,000 Rub
- www.bolshoi.ru

Top 10 Features

1. Apollo in the Chariot of the Sun
2. Auditorium
3. Beethoven Hall
4. Portico
5. Imperial Box
6. Chandelier
7. Apollo and the Nine Muses
8. New Bolshoy Theatre
9. Historic Premieres
10. Historic Events

Apollo in the Chariot of the Sun

A striking bronze portrayal of Apollo, the God of art, and four flying horses *(above)* has crowned the Bolshoy's grand portico since 1825. The sculpture also features on the rear of the 100-rouble note.

Auditorium

The auditorium, with five elaborate tiers of boxes, has a capacity of 2,150. The decorative scheme features crimson draping, white stucco mouldings and copious amounts of gold leaf; its restoration in 1976 required 6 kg (13 lb) of gold.

Beethoven Hall

Opened in 1920 to celebrate Beethoven's 150th anniversary, this hall *(below)* boasts stuccoed decoration on the ceiling, and walls lined with silk panels.

Portico
4 The stately portico with its eight Ionic columns *(above)* was part of the 1825 design envisaged by Chief Architect of Moscow city centre, Osip Bove.

Imperial Box
5 Hung with crimson velvet, the lavish royal box *(centre)* dominates the rear of the hall. Above the box, Russia's imperial crown has replaced the Soviet hammer and sickle.

Chandelier
6 Imported from France in 1863, the 1.5-tonne (3,300-lb) cut-glass chandelier had its candles replaced by 300 electric light bulbs in 1895.

Apollo and the Nine Muses
7 Encircling the central chandelier is a splendid segmented ceiling fresco featuring portraits of Apollo and the nine creative muses *(above)*. It was painted in 1856 and has since been restored.

New Bolshoy Theatre
8 The New Bolshoy *(below)*, adjacent to the original, was built in a record-breaking six months to host performances while the main theatre is being renovated.

Historic Premieres
9 Among the major premieres staged at the Bolshoy were Tchaikovsky's *Swan Lake* (1877), Rachmaninoff's *Aleko* (1893) and Glinka's *Ruslan and Ludmila* (1842).

Historic Events
10 In 1918 Lenin subdued opposition from the Left Socialist Revolutionaries by briefly imprisoning 400 of their delegates here.

Renovations 2005–11

Closed since 2005 for a long overdue restoration project, the theatre is due to re-open by 2011. Structural renovation includes sinking deeper foundations to combat subsidence caused by the underground Neglinnaya river. There will also be an overhaul of the auditorium's acoustics, which were severely impaired by poorly executed repairs during Communism.

Osip Bove also designed Teatralnaya Ploshchad (Theatre Square), in Tverskaya, which until then had been a marshy wasteland.

🔟 Tretyakov Gallery

Starting life in 1856, when Pavel Tretyakov first exhibited his collection of paintings in his front room, the Tretyakov Gallery has since evolved into the world's largest repository of Russian art, with more than 130,000 works. Tretyakov envisioned a gallery for ordinary citizens that would cover the entire spectrum of Russian art. The collection begins with ancient icons painted by anonymous masters, and ends with colourful pre-Revolution works inspired by Fauvism and later condemned by the Communists as degenerate. Works dating from the early 20th century are shown at the nearby New Tretyakov.

A portrait of Pavel Tretyakov, Tretyakov Gallery

Top 10 Features

1. Pavel Tretyakov
2. Icon Collection
3. The Peredvizhniki
4. Initial Expansion
5. Museum Church of St Nicholas in Tolmachi
6. Portrait Collection
7. Treasury
8. Main Façade
9. New Tretyakov
10. Future Expansion

🅒 Don't be put off by the long queue that often forms outside the entrance at weekends. Groups of around 30 people are let in every 15–20 minutes, so visitors should not have to wait too long.

🅓 The gallery has a great café in the basement serving meals and Russian pastries. There is also a restaurant upstairs.

- Map N5
- Ulitsa Lavrushinskiy 10
- (495) 951 1362
- Metro: Tretyakovskaya, Novokuznetskaya
- Open 10am–7:30pm Tue–Sun (museum), noon–4pm Tue–Sun (church)
- Adm: 250 Rub
- www.tretyakovgallery.ru

Pavel Tretyakov
A wealthy banker, Pavel Tretyakov (1832–98) was passionate about Russian art. His brother Sergey, meanwhile, sought out Western works. By the time of Pavel's death, they had collected over 1,600 works.

Icon Collection
The gallery houses several major icon collections *(see p22)*, including works by Dionysius *(above)* and Rublev. It catalogued and restored numerous icons found in churches closed by the Soviet regime.

The Peredvizhniki
Known as "The Wanderers", this group of late-19th-century artists organized travelling shows to bring art to the provinces. The Peredvizhniki were dedicated to depicting everyday Russian life. Members included Ilya Repin, Isaak Levitan and Vasiliy Surikov.

Initial Expansion
By 1872 the Tretyakov art collection had outgrown the family mansion and the building was extended. After Pavel's death, the family moved out and their former quarters were incorporated into the gallery.

5 Museum Church of St Nicholas in Tolmachi

Connected to the main building, this church also serves as a museum. Its highlights include the imposing 17th-century, five-tiered iconostasis and the Vladimir Icon of the Mother of God *(see p22)*, one of Russia's holiest relics.

6 Portrait Collection

Tretyakov set out to create a portrait gallery of eminent Russians and began commissioning and collecting portraits in the 1860s. Leo Tolstoy was one of the subjects.

7 Treasury

The treasury houses religious exhibits dating from the 12th century, including icon frames and a number of ancient bibles and manuscripts with ornate bindings.

8 Main Façade

In 1902 the Russian painter and graphic artist Viktor Vasnetsov remodelled the gallery's façade *(centre)*, which centres upon a relief of St George.

9 New Tretyakov

Although housed in an uninspiring concrete block, the New Tretyakov Gallery *(see p89)* has a stunning range of paintings and sculptures *(above)*. These together comprise what is today the world's best collection of Soviet art.

10 Future Expansion

In 2008 the gallery's director, Valentin Rodionov, announced plans to double the original gallery's exhibition space and renovate the New Tretyakov building *(above)*. The state has refused to help fund the gallery's 6.5-million Rub (€150-million) expansion project, but Russia's philanthropic oligarchs are expected to cover the cost.

Gallery Orientation

The Tretyakov Gallery has 62 rooms on two floors. On entering, visitors descend to the lower lobby for the ticket office and cloakrooms before climbing the main stairs to the gallery's first floor, where the chronological exhibition of paintings begins in Room 1. Steps lead down from the east wing to the ground floor, where the exhibition continues towards the treasury from Room 55 onwards.

Left **Façade of the New Tretyakov Gallery** Right *Ivan the Terrible and His Son Ivan* by Ilya Repin

TOP 10 Tretyakov Artists

1 Icon Collection – Theophanes the Greek

An ascetic monk, Theophanes produced Byzantine icons in Moscow and Novgorod in the 14th century. *The Transfiguration* and *The Dormition* are typical of his geometrical compositions.

2 Icon Collection – Dionysius

Dionysius, a renowned 15th-century icon painter, is considered to be the founder of the Moscow school of icon painting. *The Crucifixion* conveys his desire to depict spiritual perfection.

3 Icon Collection – Andrey Rublev

Trained by Theophanes, Rublev is revered as one of Russia's greatest icon painters. In the simple composition *The Trinity*, he skilfully depicts the three angels who visited Abraham.

The Trinity by Andrey Rublev

4 Icon Collection – Vladimir Icon of the Mother of God

This 12th-century icon, with its haunting image of the Virgin Mary, is among Russia's most venerated relics. It is credited with saving Moscow from attack on several occasions.

5 Icon Collection – Pskov School of Icon Painting

Pskov's icon painters developed a style characterized by a poetic and colourful approach to their subjects, as seen in the simple yet effective colour contrasts of *Saints Boris and Gleb*.

6 Vrubel Collection

Russia's foremost Symbolist artist, Mikhail Vrubel (1856–1910) painted the monumental *Princess of the Dream*, which covers an entire wall. Among his works is a ceramic fireplace, *Volga and Mikula*.

7 Bryullov Collection

The works of Karl Bryullov (1799–1852) are dominated by the vast *Siege of Pskov* (1831–43), which depicts Russian priests marching against Polish and Lithuanian soldiers in 1581.

8 Levitan Collection

Isaak Levitan (1860–1900) was fascinated by wide vistas and conveyed mood through land-scapes such as *Whirlpool* (1892). The desolate *Vladimir Road* (1894) depicts the rough track trodden by convicts destined for Siberia.

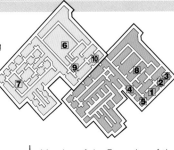

9 Repin Collection

One of the most moving works by "the Wanderer" Ilya Repin (1844–1930) is *Ivan the Terrible and His Son Ivan* (1885), which captures Ivan the Terrible's horror as he realizes he has killed his beloved son.

10 Surikov Collection

Another "Wanderer", Vasiliy Surikov (1848–1916) was a master of historic compositions. The *Morning of the Execution of the Streltsy* (1881) depicts chaotic, emotional scenes filled with a range of fascinating characters.

Top Ten Works of Art

1. *Bathing the Red Horse* (1912) by Kuzma Petrov-Vodkin (1878–1939)
2. *By the Sea. A Family* (1962–4) by Dmitry Zhilinsky (b. 1927)
3. *A Letter from the Front* (1947) by Alexander Lationov (1910–72)
4. *Josef Stalin and Kliment Voroshilov* (1938) by Alexander Gerasimov (1881–1963)
5. *The Worker and the Collective Farmer* (1936) by Vera Mukhina (1899–1953)
6. *Future Pilots* (1938) by Alexander Deyneka (1899–1969)
7. *Sakko and Vanzetti* (1927) by Alexander Tyshler (1898–1980)
8. *Above the Town* (1914–18) by Marc Chagall (1887–1985)
9. *The Dim* (1917) by Vasily Kandinsky (1866–1944)
10. *Black Suprematic Square* (1915) by Kazimir Malevich (1878–1935)

New Tretyakov Gallery

The New Tretyakov Gallery is a 15-minute walk away, housed in the Central House of Artists (see p38). The gallery collection is arranged chronologically, starting with early 20th-century works, such as Bathing the Red Horse, *a bold piece by Symbolist painter Kuzma Petrov-Vodkin, and progressing towards the Russian Revolution of 1917 and beyond. During Communism the State strongly supported those artists who produced idealistic Socialist Realism pieces, which "the masses could understand and appreciate". Many other artistic movements, particularly the avant-garde and, later, Conceptualism, were suppressed and their exponents persecuted. It was not until the collapse of the Soviet Union that gallery curators could show the true scope of 20th-century Soviet art by exhibiting the New Tretyakov's unsurpassed collection of mainstream and underground works side by side.*

Bathing the Red Horse by Kuzma Petrov-Vodkin

For information on other galleries in Moscow **See pp38–9.**

Metro Stations

Opened in 1935 as part of the government's plan to transform Moscow into the world's capital of Communism, the metro's first stations were conceived as magnificent showcases of Soviet success. Thousands of labourers and genuinely patriotic volunteers dug the tunnels, initially using simple pickaxes and shovels. Today, retaining ubiquitous red stars and original Soviet artworks, the metro is a working museum of Communist design. The system carries 7 million passengers a day and currently has 177 stations on 12 lines.

Kropotkinskaya metro station

🔾 To help passengers with orientation, a male voice announces stations on trains travelling west–east/ north–south, while a female announcer is used for east–west/ south–north trains.

🍴 Kiosks serving drinks and hot snacks are usually located in the transit passages between stations.

• Map: D2 (Mayakovskaya); N3 (Ploshchad Revolyutsii); L5 (Kropotkinskaya); M2 (Teatralnaya); G1 (Komsomolskaya); R6 (Taganskaya); C4 (Kievskaya); P5 (Novokuznetskaya); E1 (Novoslobodskaya); L4 (Arbatskaya)
• Open 5:30–1am
• http://engl. mosmetro.ru

Top 10 Features

1. Mayakovskaya
2. Ploshchad Revolutsii
3. Kropotkinskaya
4. Teatralnaya
5. Komsomolskaya
6. Taganskaya
7. Kievskaya
8. Novokuznetskaya
9. Novoslobodskaya
10. Arbatskaya

1 Mayakovskaya (1938)
One of the world's most beautiful metro stations, Mayakovskaya has Art Deco styling and is famous for its 35 superb ceiling mosaics depicting "24 Hours in the Land of the Soviets". It won a grand prize at the 1938 New York World Trade Fair.

2 Ploshchad Revolyutsii (1938)
Stalin's favourite station, Ploshchad Revolyutsii has niches containing 80 life-size bronze sculptures *(above)* of Soviet citizens. Students rub the noses of the bronze guard dogs for luck before sitting exams.

3 Kropotkinskaya (1935)
Envisaged as the station for the unrealized Palace of the Soviets, Kropotkinskaya was designed to be grand. The central hall has a single broad ceiling supported by two rows of columns.

4 Teatralnaya (1938)
Intended to celebrate culture and the creative arts, the station ceiling is adorned with exquisite porcelain figures depicting dancing men and women from seven of the eleven Soviet republics, all in traditional dress.

By 2015, 43 new stations are due to be added to Moscow's metro system.

Komsomolskaya (1952)

This Baroque-style station *(centre)* has more Communist memorabilia than most. It boasts a bust of Lenin, a delightful mosaic of Lenin addressing a rally outside the Kremlin, and a domed hall with a massive red mosaic star.

Taganskaya (1950)

Taganskaya *(above)* has supporting pylons lined with white marble, each adorned with a ceramic relief depicting a Soviet hero against a sky-blue background.

Kievskaya (1954)

This elegant station, which was designed to illustrate Russia's friendship with Ukraine, features massive Ionic-styled pylons adorned with imitation mosaics *(below)* that depict idyllic scenes of Ukrainian life.

Metro 2 – The Kremlin Line

Although its existence has never been confirmed or denied, most Muscovites believe that, in the 1950s, Stalin ordered the construction of Metro 2, a top-secret line dug deeper than the civilian metro system, intended to link the Kremlin to Vnukovo airport and a network of nuclear bunkers. Branch lines are thought to have been added to connect the Central Committee building, secret locations and civilian buildings, such as Moscow State University (see p97).

Novokuznetskaya (1943)

Built during World War II, this magnificent station was intended as a celebration of Russian military prowess and includes dramatic bronze portraits of heroic leaders and some fine ceiling mosaics.

Novoslobodskaya (1952)

Novoslobodskaya is famous for its back-lit stained-glass panels, made by Latvian artists, depicting Soviet citizens.

Arbatskaya (1953)

Arbatskaya station *(left)* is on the Arbatsko-Pokrovskaya line, one of the longest and deepest on the metro. Its graceful central hall has a high vaulted ceiling with elaborate ornamentation.

🔟 Novodevichiy Convent

This splendid UNESCO-listed convent was founded in 1525 to celebrate Grand Prince Basil III's recapture of Smolensk in 1514. Many aristocrats took their vows here and it became known as a nunnery of nobility. Tsarevna Sophia Alexeyevna (1657–1704), who served as a transitional ruler of Russia, ordered the reconstruction of many of the buildings in Moscow Baroque style, with fine ornamentation. The convent was occupied in 1812 by Napoleon's troops, and later used as a female prison before becoming a museum during Communism.

Lopukhin Palace

🔵 The churches are only open during services: 8–10am and 5–7pm.

Maps of the Novodevichiy Cemetery are available at the entrance of the cemetery.

🔵 The kiosks around Sportivnaya metro station are the closest source of refreshments.

- Map B6
- Novodevichiy proezd 1
- (495) 246 8526
- Metro: Sportivnaya
- Open 8am–7pm Wed–Mon (convent complex); 10am–5pm Wed–Mon (museums). The Cathedral of Our Lady of Smolensk is open only in summer (Apr–Oct).
- Adm: 150 Rub
- www.shm.ru

Top 10 Features

1. Irina Gudunova Chambers Museum
2. Cathedral of Our Lady of Smolensk
3. Cathedral Frescoes
4. Church of the Transfiguration
5. Six-Tiered Bell Tower
6. Lopukhin Palace
7. Streltsy Guardhouse Museum
8. Mariinsky Chambers
9. Novodevichiy Cemetery
10. Famous Graves

Irina Gudunova Chambers Museum

After the death of Tsar Fyodor I (1557–98), his wife Irina entered the convent. Her chambers are now filled with some of the precious treasures and icons bestowed upon Novodevichiy by its wealthy inhabitants.

Cathedral of Our Lady of Smolensk

Similar in design to the Kremlin's Cathedral of the Assumption (see pp12–13), this cathedral has high ceilings that enhance its spacious interior (centre). It was consecrated in 1525. The radiant five-tiered iconostasis was donated to the cathedral by Tsarevna Sophia in 1685.

Cathedral Frescoes

Painted in the mid-16th century, the frescoes depict biblical figures as well as the Russian princes and holy warriors who brought glory at Smolensk.

Church of the Transfiguration

The pretty church, with its five small golden domes (left), was built on a platform above the northern gate in 1688. It is currently used by the resident metropolitan (bishop) for private worship.

Among the exhibits at the Irina Gudunova Chambers Museum are the burial iconostases of Sophia Alexeyevna and her sisters.

5 Six-Tiered Bell Tower

Erected in 1689, the elegant 72-m- (236-ft-) high bell tower *(left)* is a brilliant example of Moscow Baroque. It originally had chapels on both the ground and first floors, and bells on the third and fifth tiers.

6 Lopukhin Palace

Peter I confined his first wife Tsarina Eudoxia Lopukhina here in 1728. The building was later occupied by Mother Superiors and is now the Metropolitan's residence.

7 Streltsy Guardhouse Museum

Positioned beneath Naprudnaya Tower for use by the convent's Streltsy guards, this low stone building now displays ancient icons and churchware *(above)*.

8 Mariinsky Chambers

Built over four floors with rows of tiny windows, the Mariinskiy Chambers are believed to have been the residence of Tsarevna Sophia until her death in 1704.

9 Novodevichiy Cemetery

Opened in 1898 due to a lack of space within the convent, the cemetery *(below)* soon became the burial place of choice for Russia's leading cultural figures and politicians.

10 Famous Graves

Anton Chekhov, interred here in 1904, was one of the first of the cemetery's illustrious residents. Among those who followed him are the writer Mikhail Bulgakov, (1940), film director Sergei Eisenstein (1948), Nikita Khrushchev (1971) and Boris Yeltsin (2007).

Unwanted Women

Though it was common practice in Russia for noble women to retire to convents, some were sent against their will. Peter the Great's first wife, Eudoxia Lopukhina, suffered this fate, as did Tsarevna Sophia, who was forced to enter the convent in 1689. In 1698, following two unsuccessful revolts, Sophia was condemned to solitary confinement for the rest of her life.

There are 27,000 graves at Novodevichiy Cemetery, many featuring remarkable headstones and memorial sculptures.

🔟 Kolomenskoe Estate

Set in idyllic riverside parkland, Kolomenskoe was the favourite summer residence of Ivan the Terrible and was also popular with Tsar Mikhail I (1596–1645). Both leaders made improvements, but it was Tsar Alexei (1629–76) who decided to build his "country Kremlin" here. A fine wooden palace, with an eclectic ensemble of buildings and 270 lavishly furnished rooms, was created in 1667. After Alexei's death the palace fell into disrepair and was demolished by Catherine the Great (1729–96). Today the estate draws Muscovites, who come to picnic, sledge and attend festivals in the grounds.

An artistic impression of the Kolomenskoe Estate

🚩 Kolomenskoe is a lovely spot for a ride by *troika* (horse drawn buggy) in both summer and winter.

🍴 Log cabins serving drinks and grilled snacks can be found at the western end of the estate.

• Map B3
• Andropova Prospekt 39
• (495) 115 2768
• Metro: Kolomenskaya
• Open Apr–Oct: 8am–10pm Tue–Sun; Nov–Mar: 8am–9pm (grounds); 10am–5pm (exhibition)
• Adm: 150 Rub (exhibition)
• www.mgomz.ru

Top 10 Features

1. Pavilion Palace
2. Frjazhsky Cellars
3. Front Gatehouse
4. Kolomenskoe Museum
5. Festivals
6. Church of the Ascension
7. Gardens
8. Church of Our Lady of Kazan
9. Peter the Great's Wooden Cabin
10. Stable Yard

1 Pavilion Palace
The only surviving records of Tsar Alexei's fairytale wooden palace are engravings and a superb scale model *(above)*, which is displayed in the modern Pavilion Palace, where the wooden structure once stood.

2 Frjazhsky Cellars
Part of the group of buildings adjoining the front gatehouse, the Frjazhsky Cellars were once used to store the royal wine collection. They have now been restored and are used to host receptions and banquets.

3 Front Gatehouse
This 1684 gate *(left)* is one of the estate's oldest surviving buildings. The larger arch was for horse traffic, while the smaller one was used by pedestrians. By the gate were two mechanical lions, which would roar when visitors entered.

Kolomenskaya
900 metres
(1000 yards)
Entrance

Kolomenskoe Museum

This museum includes church bells *(right)*, leather-bound books and manuscripts and wood carvings from neglected monasteries and estates in the Moscow region.

Festivals

Kolomenskoe hosts a number of annual festivals including Victory Day (9 May). Peter the Great's Birthday (30 May) and Moscow Day (6 Sep) are both celebrated with colourful medieval processions.

Church of the Ascension

This UNESCO-listed church *(below)* was erected to honour the birth of Ivan the Terrible in 1530. It was the first stone structure to include a tented roof, designed to prevent snow piling up.

Gardens

Apple, pear and cherry trees fill the 17th-century Voznesenski and Kazanski gardens; the nearby kitchen garden once supplied fresh vegetables to the palace. Ancient oak trees surround Peter the Great's wooden cabin.

Church of Our Lady of Kazan

Built in the mid-17th century to mark Moscow's liberation from Poland, this church *(centre)* features blue domes adorned with golden stars. It was originally linked to Tsar Alexei's wooden palace by a walkway.

Peter the Great's Wooden Cabin

Among the buildings collected for the Museum of Wooden Architecture during the 20th century is a log cabin *(right)* from Arkhangelsk (on Russia's north coast). Peter the Great stayed in the cabin while overseeing the formation of the Russian navy in 1698.

Stable Yard

Tucked away on the eastern side of the estate is a small reconstructed village with stables and caged hawks, where costumed guides give talks and entertain children.

Toy Soldiers

At the age of ten, Peter the Great moved to Kolomenskoe and pursued his interest in military tactics by playing war games with regiments of real soldiers. Seven years later, he foiled a plot by his half-sister Tsarevna Sophia using the loyal soldiers that he had trained as a child.

Left **Boris Yeltsin** Right **An artistic impression of Moscow in flames in 1812**

Moments in Moscow's History

1 First Recorded Reference
Moscow was first mentioned in the *Ipatievskaya Chronicles* of 1147 when Kiev was the capital of Russia. Moscow was then a minor outpost, reputedly founded by Prince Yuri Dolguruki.

2 Mongol Invasion
In 1237–8, the fledgling town was burned to the ground and its denizens massacred by Mongol armies under Batu Khan. Under the Mongols, Russian principalities were left to govern themselves and Moscow grew into a powerful city.

3 Reign of Ivan the Great
When Ivan the Great became Grand Prince of Moscow in 1462, the city gained in power and Russian territory was expanded.

Ivan the Great Bell Tower complex, Kremlin

This eventually enabled him to wrest Russia from Mongol control. To celebrate, he invited Italian architects to remodel the Kremlin in 1472.

4 Polish-Muscovite War
In the course of this war (1605–18), Polish and Lithuanian troops succeeded in occupying Moscow in 1610. In 1612 they were routed after Russian volunteer troops from Novgorod, led by Prince Pozharskiy and Kuzma Minin, laid siege to the Kremlin.

5 Capital Relocated
Peter the Great loathed Moscow and in 1713 he moved Russia's capital to his newly constructed city of St Petersburg. Tsars continued to be crowned in Moscow and the city remained culturally and commercially active.

6 Moscow Burns
In 1812 Napoleon conquered Moscow and made a victorious speech on Red Square, but Muscovites set the city ablaze as he advanced and his troops were left without shelter or supplies. As winter set in, Napoleon's army was forced to retreat.

7 Capital Returns
As German forces advanced on St Petersburg in 1918, Lenin feared the collapse of the Bolshevik Revolution and moved Russia's seat of government to Moscow. It was not declared the official capital until 1922.

Preceding pages **Ballerinas performing Tchaikovsky's** *Swan Lake* **at the Bolshoy Theatre**

"Defend Moscow", a 1941 propaganda poster

Top 10 Great Russian Leaders

1 Dmitriy Donskoy (1359–89)
The first Grand Prince to defeat the Mongols, he built the first stone Kremlin.

2 Ivan the Great (1462–1505)
A powerful leader, he consolidated Russian territory and won freedom from the Mongols.

3 Ivan the Terrible (1547–84)
A formidable leader, his victory at Kazan in 1552 pushed the Mongols further back.

4 Prince Dmitriy Pozharskiy (1578–1642)
Together with Kuzma Minin, Prince Pozharskiy put an end to Russian instability by clearing enemy troops from the Kremlin in 1612.

5 Peter the Great (1682–1725)
This visionary leader created St Petersburg and modernized Russia along Western lines.

6 Catherine the Great (1762–96)
She was respected for her enlightened approach to Russia's modernization.

7 Alexander II (1855–81)
He abolished serfdom and capital punishment.

8 Vladimir Lenin (1917–24)
The orchestrator of the 1917 Bolshevik Revolution and first leader of the USSR.

9 Joseph Stalin (1927–53)
His paranoid purges led to the execution or exile of millions of Soviet citizens.

10 Vladimir Putin (2000–2008)
His leadership brought some stability to Russia.

8 German Invasion
Hitler's invasion of Russia in 1941 took Stalin by surprise. In just a few months, German troops were within 20 km (12 miles) of Moscow. The city was saved by a severe winter for which the invading troops were unprepared.

9 USSR Dissolved
While Mikhail Gorbachev remained President of the Soviet Union, Boris Yeltsin was democratically elected as President of the Russian Federation in June 1991. When hard-line Communists attempted to oust Gorbachev in August 1991, Yeltsin foiled the coup. In the following months he orchestrated the dissolution of the Soviet Union; Gorbachev resigned on 24 December and the Soviet Union ceased to exist.

10 Dubrovka Theatre Siege
In 2002, in this most notorious of several terrorist attacks on Moscow, the theatre and its 850 audience members were seized by Chechen separatists who demanded Russia's withdrawal from Chechnya. In a poorly managed rescue attempt, 39 of the terrorists were killed along with 129 hostages.

Left **Archaeological Museum** Right **A display at the Museum of Modern History**

Museums

Gorky House Museum

Designed by Fyodor Shekhtel for millionaire banker Stepan Ryabushinskiy in 1900, this house is Moscow's finest example of Art Nouveau architecture and features wonderfully organic styling and flowing floral motifs, of which the highlight is an Estonian limestone staircase. The house was presented by Stalin to the writer Maxim Gorky in 1931 and today serves as a museum displaying his personal effects, letters and manuscripts *(see p85)*.

Polytechnical Museum

This museum's fascinating themed exhibits include a wonderful selection of Soviet-era electronic equipment, such as early televisions, synthesizers and gramophones. The basement houses antique vehicles from Russia and abroad *(see p71)*.

Matryoshka Museum

The art collector Andrey Mamontov is credited with producing the first *matryoshka* dolls in 1890. His 19th-century workshop is now occupied by the Matryoshka Museum, with an enchanting array of dolls from the 20th century. It is also the best place to buy a high-quality souvenir doll. ◈ Map L2 • *Leontievskiy pereulok 7* • *(495) 291 9645* • *Metro: Tverskaya, Pushkinskaya* • *Open 10am–6pm Mon–Thu, 11am–7pm Sat–Sun*

A *matryoshka* doll, Matryoshka Museum

State Armoury

This peerless collection of Russian treasures has been amassed over the past 800 years. Antique armour and weaponry compete with the glittering paraphernalia that accompanied royal coronations and weddings, such as extravagantly ornamented thrones, bejewelled crowns, lavish ceremonial dress and glittering icons *(see pp14–15)*.

Historical Museum

With its Russian Revival decor restored to dazzling splendour, this museum provides a stunning backdrop to its extensive collection of ancient

A model of a nuclear reactor, Polytechnical Museum

Matryoshka are among Russia's most popular souvenirs. These dolls fit one inside the other and come in a huge variety of styles.

Stately façade of the Historical Museum

manuscripts, imperial carriages and sledges, aristocratic fashion and the country's largest exhibition of coins *(see p63)*.

6 Museum of Modern History

This excellent museum is housed in a splendid 18th-century mansion. Its numerous rooms include informative displays on topics such as Russia's development from an agricultural to an industrial society, the 1917 revolution, both World Wars and space exploration *(see p83)*.

7 Museum of the Great Patriotic War

More than 20 million Soviet soldiers and civilians were lost in what Russians call the Great Patriotic War (World War II), and this vast building serves as both memorial and museum. The exhibits are arranged around the solemn Hall of Glory, inscribed with the names of the war heroes. Behind the museum is an exhibition of military vehicles *(see p95)*.

8 Archaeological Museum

Set 8 m (26 ft) underground, this museum gives visitors the chance to delve beneath the city's surface. It is built around the 16th-century foundations of the Voskresenkiy Bridge, which were unearthed along with other artifacts during construction work in 1994 *(see p70)*.

9 Mayakovsky Museum

This museum, dedicated to the life and work of the Futurist artist and poet Vladimir Mayakovsky, is housed in the flat that he shared with his fellow artists. Mayakovsky's manuscripts, artwork and personal belongings are exhibited throughout all four floors of the building *(see p69)*.

10 Tolstoy House Museum

Tolstoy's incredibly well-preserved winter residence offers an evocative glimpse into the writer's comfortable life with his wife Sophia and their nine children. The house contains the family's original furniture and visitors can view the upstairs study where Tolstoy wrote *Resurrection*, among other works *(see p97)*.

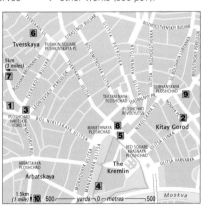

Left **Epiphany Cathedral** Right **Iconostasis, Church of the Trinity in Nikitniki**

🔟 Churches and Cathedrals

1 St Basil's Cathedral
Moscow's enchanting landmark cathedral has eight small chapels, all connected by a beautifully tiled gallery and centred on a tent-roofed tower that rises gracefully above their colourful onion domes *(see pp8–9)*.

2 Cathedral of the Assumption
Designed in 1497 by Italian architect Aristotle Fioravanti, this cathedral is a remarkable combination of Russian Orthodox and Renaissance architectural features. With its interior completely covered with 16th-century frescoes, it was a fitting site for the sumptuous coronation and wedding ceremonies of Russia's royalty *(see pp12–13)*.

Tiled gallery, St Basil's Cathedral

3 Cathedral of the Archangel
This striking limestone cathedral, topped by a bulbous golden dome, was designed by a Venetian architect in 1505 and combines Western and Eastern architectural motifs. It was used for the burials of Moscow's tsars and princes until the 18th century *(see p66)*.

4 Cathedral of Christ the Saviour
A replica of the 19th-century original, this magnificent cathedral was opened in 2000. It took ten years to reconstruct, and came in at a final cost of more than £103 million (5 billion Rub) *(see p75)*.

5 Church of St Gregory of Neocaesarea
The delightful Church of St Gregory of Neocaesarea inspired Napoleon to remark in 1812 that he regretted he could not take all of Moscow's beautiful churches back to Paris. Built in the late 17th century, it is crowned with silver onion domes and the tent-roofed bell tower extends onto the pavement *(see p91)*.

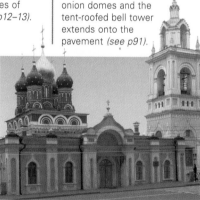

The striking Church of St Gregory of Neocaesarea

Colourful Kazan Cathedral

9 Transfiguration Cathedral

Part of the Novospasskiy monastic complex (see p97), this cathedral was founded in 1491 and rebuilt in 1645 with tall arched gables to resemble the Cathedral of the Assumption. During the Soviet era the monastery was used as a concentration camp, orphanage and furniture factory; the church interior was damaged, but restoration is under way. Surviving frescoes depict biblical scenes, Greek philosophers and Russian royals. ❂ Map G5 • Krestyanskaya Ploshchad • Metro: Proletarskaya • Open 8am–8pm

6 Kazan Cathedral

This remarkable cathedral was rebuilt in 1993 after the original 17th-century church was demolished by Stalin in 1936 to give parading soldiers better access to Red Square. It was first built to honour the miraculous Icon of the Kazan Virgin, a replica of which is on display inside. ❂ Map M3 • Krasnaya Ploshchad • (495) 298 0131 • Metro: Okhotnyy Ryad • Open 8am–8pm

7 Epiphany Cathedral

This cathedral boasts lavish white ornamentation typical of the Moscow Baroque style. Its small golden dome is supported by a broad hexagonal drum. The restored interior is dominated by a bright gilt iconostasis, which rises into the main tower (see p69).

8 Church of the Trinity in Nikitniki

Flanked by chapels and a tent-roofed bell tower, this is a masterpiece of 17th-century church architecture. The interior contains a superb ornate iconostasis and is covered with original frescoes (see p69).

10 Church of the Resurrection in Kadashi

The interior of the 17th-century Church of the Resurrection in Kadashi is currently being restored, but the façade is as striking as ever. Its ostentatious limestone decoration is a classic example of Moscow Baroque, as is the elegant tapering bell tower (see p89).

Left **Main entrance, Tretyakov Gallery** Right **Contemporary art exhibition, Winzavod**

🔟 Art Galleries

1 Tretyakov Gallery
An unrivalled collection of pre-1917 Russian art fills over 60 rooms in this labyrinthine gallery. Exhibits include medieval icons, jewellery and church treasures, as well as paintings, drawings and sculptures from every period of Russian history *(see pp20–23)*.

2 Central House of Artists
Occupying the same faceless concrete block as the New Tretyakov Gallery, the Central House of Artists comprises numerous shops and private galleries exhibiting everything from hand-made jewellery to photography and ceramics. The main hall hosts temporary exhibitions and a small cinema regularly screens international art-house films *(see p92)*.

Greek marble sarcophagus, Pushkin Museum of Fine Arts

3 Pushkin Museum of Fine Arts
This grand museum boasts one of Russia's best collections of European art, including plaster casts of classical and Renaissance sculptures, ancient Egyptian portraits and the 4,500-year-old Troy Treasure *(see pp16–17)*.

4 New Tretyakov Gallery
This gallery features some of the best Soviet art of the 20th century. Highlights include Modernist works by Marc Chagall, Kazimir Malevich and Vasily Kandinsky, as well as monumental works of Socialist Realism by artists such as Alexander Gerasimov *(see p89)*.

5 Glazunov Gallery
Housed in a 19th-century mansion, the Glazunov is packed with atmospheric landscapes and

Paintings and antiques on display at the Central House of Artists

The opulent mansion housing the Glazunov Gallery

portraits by Ilya Glazunov (b. 1930), director of Russia's Academy of Painting, Sculpture and Architecture. ⌦ *Map L5 • Ulitsa Volkhonka 13 • (495) 291 6949 • Metro: Kropotkinskaya • Open 11am–7pm Tue–Sun • Adm • www.glazunov.ru*

Winzavod

One of Moscow's trendiest contemporary art centres, Winzavod comprises nine stylish exhibition spaces in a converted winery. ⌦ *Map H3 • 4 Syromyatnicheskiy pereulok 1, Bldg 6 • (495) 917 4646 • Metro: Chkalovskaya • Open noon–8pm Tue–Sun • www.winzavod.com*

Moscow House of Photography

This collection of 70,000-plus prints and negatives ranges from 19th-century daguerreotypes to modern digital photographs. ⌦ *Map K5 • Ulitsa Sushchevskaya 14 • (495) 231 3325 • Metro: Novoslobodskaya • Open 11am–8pm Tue–Sun • www.mdf.ru*

Pop/Off/Art

Established in 2004, this gallery represents over 30 Russian artists and exhibits a broad range of contemporary paintings, sculptures, installations and photographs. ⌦ *Map H2 • Ulitsa Radio 6/4 • (499) 261 7883 • Metro: Kurskaya • Open noon–8pm Mon–Sat • www.popoffart.com*

Marat Guelman Gallery

One of the first private galleries to open in post-Communist Russia, the Marat Guelman Gallery quickly gained a reputation for its ability to spot emerging artistic talent. Today it is among the main contemporary art centres in the country *(see p92)*.

Museum of Modern Art

Opened by influential Moscow arts patron Zurab Tsereteli, the Museum of Modern Art has a collection of Soviet art to rival that of the New Tretyakov. Occupying a large mansion, it also exhibits a broad range of Western art and has a courtyard filled with intriguing sculptures *(see p83)*.

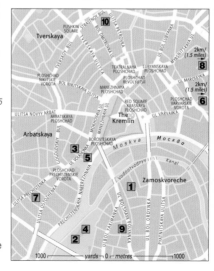

The Moscow House of Photography hosts regular exhibitions of works by both Russian and international photographers.

Left **Tchaikovsky Concert Hall** Right **Moscow International Performing Arts Centre**

Performing Arts Venues

1 Moscow International Performing Arts Centre

Opened in 2002, this cylindrical glass building houses two concert halls and a theatre. State-of-the-art facilities include the 1,700-seat Svetlanov Hall, which is panelled with Siberian Larch for world-class acoustics, and features Russia's largest organ. ⊗ *Map G5 • Kosmodamianskaya Emb 58 • (495) 730 1011 • Metro: Paveletskaya • Open 11am–10pm • www.mmdm.ru*

2 Bolshoy Theatre

This theatre is one of Moscow's iconic landmarks. Performances are currently being staged at the neighbouring New Bolshoy while the grand theatre undergoes renovations *(see pp18–19)*.

Tchaikovsky monument, Moscow Conservatory

Luxurious interior of the Bolshoy Theatre

3 Moscow Conservatory

This celebrated venue houses a magnificent Great Hall and four smaller chamber halls. Built in 1901, the Great Hall seats 1,700 and has excellent acoustics. The Conservatory holds regular concerts in all five venues and also organizes annual festivals. ⊗ *Map L3 • Ulitsa Bolshaya Nikitsa 13 • (495) 629 8183 • Metro: Arbatskaya, Pushkinskaya • Open 11am–7pm (ticket office) • Adm • www.mosconsv.ru*

4 Tchaikovsky Concert Hall

Conceived by theatre director Vsevolod Meierhold (1874–1940) as Moscow's largest modern theatre, this building was on the point of completion when, in 1939, he was arrested and executed during Stalin's purges. It was given to the Moscow Philharmonic Society who named it after Tchaikovsky in 1940. The 1,500-seat hall hosts regular musicals, operas and concerts. ⊗ *Map D2 • Triumfalnaya Ploshchad 4/31 • (495) 232 5353 • Metro: Mayakovskaya • Open noon–7:30pm (ticket office) • Adm • www.classicalmusic.ru*

5 New Ballet

Founded in 1989 by dancer-directors Aida Chernova and Sergei Starukhin, the New Ballet is devoted to their style of Plastic Ballet based on free movement.

 The Moscow International Performing Arts Centre is also known as the International House of Music.

Their repertoire includes dance interpretations of art by Hieronymus Bosch and music by the Symbolist composer Aleksandr Skryabin.
⑤ Map H2 • Ulitsa Novaya Basmannaya 25/2 • (495) 632 2911 • Metro: Krasnye Vorota • Open 11am–7pm (ticket office) • Adm
• www.newballet.net

Plastic Ballet performance at the New Ballet

State Kremlin Palace
6 This prestigious venue was commissioned by Nikita Khrushchev in 1961 as a congress hall for Communist Party conventions. Today the concrete and glass structure hosts major concerts, ballet and opera performances in a 6,000-seat hall. ⑤ Map M4 • Kremlin • (495) 628 5232 • Metro: Borovitskaya, Biblioteka im. Lenina • Open noon–8pm (ticket office)

Moscow Art Theatre
7 Renowned for staging premieres of Chekhov's plays, this theatre today performs a broad repertoire of Russian and international plays (see p83).

Helikon Opera
8 Established in 1990 by Dmitry Bertman, the Helikon has earned major acclaim for its innovative opera recitals. Performances are currently being staged at an alternative venue while the opera house undergoes renovations.
⑤ Map L3 • Novyy Arbat 11 • (495) 695 6584 • Metro: Arbatskaya • Open 11am–7pm (ticket office) • Adm • www.helikon.ru

Lenkom Theatre
9 This popular venue puts on cutting-edge modern drama. Tickets often sell out weeks in advance. ⑤ Map E2 • Ulitsa Malaya Dmitrovka 6 • (495) 699 0708 • Metro: Chekhovskaya • Open 11am–7pm • Adm

Satirikon Theatre
10 Opened by renowned humourist Arkadi Raikin in 1984, this theatre stages both experimental and classic plays.
⑤ Map B1 • Ulitsa Sheremetyevskaya 8 • (495) 602 6583 • Metro: Rizhskaya • Open 11am–7pm • Adm

The State Kremlin Palace was sunk 15 m (49 ft) into the ground so as not to dwarf the neighbouring buildings.

Left **Portrait of Anton Chekhov** Right **Leo Tolstoy pictured in his study**

🔟 **Russian Writers**

1 Pushkin (1799–1837)
Regarded by many as the father of modern Russian literature, Alexander Pushkin most famously wrote *Eugene Onegin* and *Boris Godunov*, works which are still performed by Moscow's Bolshoy Opera Company.

Alexander Pushkin attending a court ball

2 Tolstoy (1828–1910)
In epic masterpieces such as *War and Peace* and *Anna Karenina*, Leo Tolstoy chronicled 19th-century Russian life with such expressive realism that he became known as one of the world's greatest writers.

3 Dostoevsky (1821–81)
Moscow-born Fyodor Dostoevsky achieved literary fame by the age of 24, but it took four years of hard labour in Siberia for his writing to mature into the dark psychological explorations that earned him a reputation as the founder of modern existentialism.

Statue of Fyodor Dostoevsky

4 Chekhov (1860–1904)
Anton Chekhov studied medicine at Moscow University and continued practising as a doctor even after he achieved literary fame for his short stories and plays. He once declared, "Medicine is my lawful wife and literature is my mistress."

5 Bulgakov (1891–1940)
Though an active novelist and playwright throughout his adult life, Mikhail Bulgakov only achieved international acclaim for his satirical novel *The Master and Margarita*, which is set in Moscow, after his death.

6 Lermontov (1814–41)
Born in Moscow to an aristocratic family, Mikhail Lermontov began writing successful poetry as a teenager, but was killed in a duel at the age of 26. Although he had only one volume published during his lifetime, he later achieved posthumous recognition for his deeply patriotic poems.

7 Turgenev (1818–83)
A contemporary of Tolstoy and Dostoevsky, Ivan Turgenev lived abroad for much of his life yet continued to write about Russian society. His most famous work, *Fathers and Sons*,

Ivan Turgenev, author of *Fathers and Sons*

is a Modernist portrayal of the widening generation gap in Russia.

Solzhenitsyn (1918–2008)

Krushchev's unexpected approval of the novel *One Day in the Life of Ivan Denisovich* brought Alexander Solzhenitsyn overnight success both in Russia and abroad. The book was based on his experiences of harsh gulag life and won him the Nobel Prize for Literature in 1970. His later works were suppressed and he was exiled in 1974.

Nabokov (1899–1977)

Born and raised in Russia, Vladimir Nabokov's aristocratic family fled the country in 1919 after the 1917 Revolution. Nabokov eventually ended up in America, where he wrote the novel *Lolita*, which brought him international fame.

Erofeyev (1938–90)

Venedikt Erofeyev became a literary legend after writing *Moskva-Petushki (Moscow Stations)* in 1969, which charts a drunkard's surreal journey across Moscow by train. Though it was immediately published abroad, within Russia it could only be obtained as *samizdat* (illegal copies) until 1989.

Top 10 Russian Composers

1 Glinka (1804–57)
Mikhail Glinka's two great operas – *Ivan Susanin* and *Ruslan and Lyudmila* – are still performed at the Bolshoy Theatre *(see pp18–19)*.

2 Mussorgsky (1839–81)
Modest Mussorgsky composed innovative works, often inspired by nationalist themes.

3 Tchaikovsky (1840–93)
Works such as *Swan Lake* and *The Nutcracker* have immortalised Pyotr Tchaikovsky as a world-famous composer.

4 Rimsky-Korsakov (1844–1908)
Nikolai Rimsky-Korsakov is best known for his orchestral work, such as *Russian Easter Festival Overture*.

5 Glazunov (1865–1936)
Conservative yet gifted, Alexander Glazunov wrote his first symphony at 16.

6 Skryabin (1872–1915)
Aleksandr Skryabin was a leading composer of Russian Symbolist works *(see p76)*.

7 Rachmaninov (1873–1943)
A world-class pianist, Sergei Rachmaninov is regarded as one of Russia's greatest Romantic composers.

8 Stravinsky (1882–1971)
Pianist, conductor and legendary composer, Igor Stravinsky was a musical revolutionary.

9 Prokofiev (1891–1953)
Sergei Prokofiev shocked audiences with his modern compositions.

10 Shostakovich (1906–75)
Dmitriy Shostakovich is known as one of the Soviet era's most talented composers.

Left **Bowling alley** Right **Exterior of the Sanduny Bath House**

🔟 Leisure Activities

Bath Houses
A bath-house session is one of the best ways to relax. The city's best baths are found at the 19th-century Sanduny Bath House, with male and female sections. Private rooms are available and masseurs are on hand for an additional fee *(see p84)*.

Boating
River cruises through central Moscow depart from Kievskaya metro station every two hours in summer, and last an hour and a half. Rowing boats can be hired in Gorky Park *(see p90)*.

Parks and Gardens
Moscow's numerous parks range from tiny residential spots, such as Patriarch's Pond in Tverskaya, to the vast wooded expanses of Izmaylovo and Sokolniki on the outskirts.

Tsaritsyno Park in autumn

Generally well maintained and well lit at night, they offer welcome respite from the relentless bustle of the city.

Cross-Country Skiing
In the winter Muscovites can be seen cross-country skiing in suburban areas and larger parks. Gorky and Sokolniki parks hire out cross-country ski equipment. Non-Russian speakers may require help as the rental process can be complicated.

Ice-Skating
Red Square hosts a temporary ice rink with skate hire in December and January. For year-round skating head for the Russki Lyod indoor rink at Gorky Park *(see p90)*. ॐ *Russki Lyod: (495) 237 0711 • Open 11am–11pm • Adm*

Cinema
There are plenty of multiplex cinemas in Moscow, of which October Cinema is the largest. For a Socialist-era cinematic experience, try Pushkinskiy Cinema. Most show Western as well as Russian films, but they may not always be screened in English or subtitled. ॐ *October Cinema: Map J3; Ulitsa Novyy Arbat 24; Metro: Arbatskaya • Pushkinskiy Cinema: Map L1; Pushkinskaya Ploshchad 2; (495) 545 0505; Metro: Chekhovskaya*

Ten Pin Bowling
Bowling has become enormously popular in Russia, largely thanks to the film

For information on the Moscow Film Festival, held each year in June, visit www.moscowfilmfestival.ru

A game of billiards

The Big Lebowski (1998). Moscow has over 40 bowling alleys. The largest is Cosmik's state-of-the-art 32-lane hall.
⊗ *Cosmik Bowling: Map D5 • Ulitsa Lva Tolstogo 18 • (495) 258 3131 • Metro: Park Kultury • Open noon–5am • Adm*

8 Billiards
Almost every bowling centre in Moscow has a billiard hall. Russian billiards is usually played on 4-m (12-ft) tables and the object of the game, known as Moscow Pyramid, is to pot 8 of the 15 white balls on the table.

9 Chess
Home to some of the world's most gifted chess players, Russia has a thriving chess culture. In summer, players gather in Gorky, Izmaylovo and Sokolniki parks to compete at outdoor tables. At the Mikhail Botvinnik Chess Centre, players of all levels compete during the week, while masters meet for tournaments on Sundays.
⊗ *Mikhail Botvinnik Chess Centre: Map K5 • Gogolevskiy Bulvar 14 • (495) 291 8627 • Metro: Kropotkinskaya • Open 4–9pm Mon–Thu, 11am–4pm Sun • Adm*

10 Football
Moscow has a vibrant football scene with five major clubs – Dinamo, Spartak, CSKA, FC Moskva and Lokomotiv. The venue that meets the highest standards is Luzhniki Stadium, which hosted the 2008 Champions League Final.
⊗ *Luzhniki Stadium: Map B6 • Luzhnetskaya nab 24 • Metro: Sportivnaya*

Top 10 Parks

1 Gorky Park
A popular park with a fairground, gardens and a boating and skating lake *(see p90)*.

2 Hermitage Garden
Central park with a theatre, restaurant and shaded seating areas. ⊗ *Map E2 • Karetnyy Ryad 1–3 • Metro: Chekhovskaya*

3 Alexander Gardens
Peaceful gardens beneath the Kremlin walls *(see p66)*.

4 Kolomenskoe Park
Hilly park planted with cherry trees. ⊗ *Map B3 • Andropova Prospekt • Metro: Kolomenskaya • Open 8am–9pm*

5 Botanical Gardens
Lovely 300-year-old gardens with thousands of roses and Japanese plants. ⊗ *Map A1 • Ulitsa Botanicheskaia 4 • Metro: VDNKh • May–Sep: 10am–8pm; Oct–Apr: 10am–4pm*

6 Izmaylovo Park
Vast wooded park with a skating lake and large outdoor market. ⊗ *Map B2 • Metro: Partizanskaya, Izmaylovskaya*

7 Sokolniki Park
Gardens, skating lake and Soviet-era exhibition pavilions. ⊗ *Map B1 • Sokolnicheskii val 1 • Metro: Sokolniki*

8 Victory Park
Neatly arranged gardens, a war memorial and the Museum of the Great Patriotic War *(see p96)*.

9 Tsaritsyno Park
Pleasant park on the city's southern outskirts. Site of Catherine the Great's unfinished Tsaritsyno Palace *(see p98)*.

10 Socialist Sculpture Park
Interesting small park filled with Socialist-era sculptures *(see pp90–91)*.

Moscow's Top 10

Soviet symbols on the façade of the Ministry of Foreign Affairs

Soviet Buildings

1 Ukraina Hotel (1950–56)
One of Stalin's Seven Sisters, this 34-floor, 1,600-room, 206-m- (676-ft-) high building is Europe's tallest hotel. Its lower tier is decorated with massive sculpted wheat sheaves – one of Ukraine's state symbols. ✆ *Map C4 • Kutuzovskiy Prospekt 2/1 • Metro: Kievskaya • www.hotelukraina.ru*

2 Ministry of Foreign Affairs (1948–53)
This astounding structure, one of the Seven Sisters, was supposedly modelled on Manhattan's skyscrapers. The 27-storey building was designed by architects Mikhail Minkus and Vladimir Gelfreikh (see p77).

3 Moscow State University (1949–53)
Situated on a hill to ensure its prominence, the main university building is the largest of Stalin's seven towers. The design is perfectly symmetrical, with four wings converging on the central tower (see p97).

4 Lenin Library (1928–60)
The Neo-Classical finish of this stately building reflects a compromise between its Constructivist and Classicist architects, who initially failed to agree on its design

The Neo-Classical Lenin Library building

in the 1920s. The library holds a copy of every book published in Russia since 1922 and now has over 40 million volumes. ✆ *Map M3 • Ulitsa Vozdvizhenka 3 • Metro: Biblioteka im. Lenina*

5 Lermontov Tower (1949–53)
Another of Stalin's Seven Sisters, this building has motifs inspired by historic Russian architecture. It was built on the site of the birthplace of the poet Lermontov (see p42). Flanked by two residential blocks, the central tower contains the Ministry of Transport Machinery offices. ✆ *Map G2 • Lermontovskaya Ploshchad 21 • Metro: Krasnye Vorota*

Moscow State University

The "Seven Sisters" are seven prominent tiered skyscrapers commissioned by Josef Stalin as symbols of Soviet greatness.

6 Vostaniya Apartment Building (1950–54)

Two of the Seven Sisters were designed as apartment blocks for the Soviet elite. The Vostaniya was reserved for scientists, cosmonauts and pilots. In recent years, the apartment blocks have suffered from ownership disputes and a lack of centralized maintenance. § Map J2 • Kudrinskaya Ploshchad • Metro: Barrikadnaya

7 Northern River Terminal (1932–37)

Topped by a bold red star, this elegant building was designed to resemble a 19th-century steamboat with fountains at either end. The symmetrical construction centres on a grand staircase leading from the main hall down to the river edge.
§ Map A1 • Leningradskoye Shosse 51
• Metro: Rechnoy Vokzal

8 Druzhba Arena (1979)

Nicknamed "The Spider" for its 28 concrete legs, the Druzhba Arena was built for the 1980 Olympics, when it was the world's largest concrete dome. Originally used for volleyball, the central area is now used for tennis and is surrounded by adjustable seating for between 1,700 and 3,500 spectators. § Map A2
• Luzhnetskaya nab. 4
• Metro: Sportivnaya

9 Monument to the Conquerors of Space (1964)

This dynamic monument intends to capture the moment a rocket hurtles into the sky, trailed by a jet stream. Its dark granite

Monument to the Conquerors of Space

base features reliefs of Soviet cosmonauts, engineers and scientists preparing for lift-off. §
Map B1 • Mira Prospekt • Metro: VDNKH

10 Begovaya Apartment Building (1965–78)

This building's multiple concrete legs and overlapping wall panels have earned it the nickname "The Centipede". With its functionality and the exposed structure of its legs and stairwells, it signifies Soviet Brutalism. § Map C1 • Ulitsa Begovaya 34–36 • Metro: Begovaya

There is a space museum underneath the Monument to the Conquerors of Space.

Left **A May Day procession** Right **Men carrying flowers on Women's Day**

🏆10 Festivals and Events

1 New Year
Muscovites have traditionally celebrated New Year at home, although some head to Red Square to hear the Kremlin bells strike midnight and witness the firework display.

2 Winter Festival
During the Winter Festival (late-Dec–early Jan) Red Square hosts an ice rink and Gorky Park has ice-sculpting displays. There are snowman contests on Ulitsa Arbat, and Troika rides and folk-dancing at Izmaylovo Park.

Firework display at New Year

3 Defenders of the Motherland Day
On 23 February, military parades and wreath-laying ceremonies take place at war memorials all over Russia. It was first celebrated as Red Army Day, to mark Lenin's replacement of the old royal army with an army of workers and peasants in 1918. Today it honours Russia's fallen soldiers.

4 Maslenitsa
The week before Lent is celebrated with seven days of pancakes and festivities. Events take place daily on Red Square, where a programme of theatre performances, acrobatics and music culminates with a parade and a firework display on Forgiveness Sunday.

5 Easter Festival
Moscow's Easter Festival began in 2002 and involves two weeks of classical concerts at locations all around the city. It concludes with a grand outdoor concert in Victory Park to celebrate Victory Day.

6 Women's Day
In 1917 food shortages turned Women's Day celebrations into anti-government protests that eventually led to the Revolution. Ever since, 8 March has been treated with great respect by Russians as a day when both husbands and sons venerate the women in their lives.

7 May Day
Traditionally celebrated with much pomp as Labour Day during the Soviet era, May Day is nowadays seen by radical groups as a chance to let off steam.

An ice octopus in Gorky Park, Ice Sculpture Festival

Victory Day parade in Red Square

8 Victory Day
One of Russia's most important national holidays, this event marks the moment when Nazi Germany surrendered to the Soviet Union and the Allies in Berlin on 9 May. Soldiers, war veterans and civilians join enormous parades at Red Square and Victory Park.

9 Moscow City Day
Held on the first weekend of September, City Day was created by Boris Yeltsin in 1986 to celebrate the birthday of Moscow, which began life as a small fortress in 1147. On the Saturday, colourful floats parade along Ulitsa Tverskyaka towards Red Square and there are funfairs and market stalls.

10 Day of Reconciliation
Now held on 7 November, this official holiday started out as Great October Revolution Day, and today it is only celebrated by the Communist Party. Stalinist pensioners can be seen waving portraits of "Uncle Joe" in front of the Lenin Mausoleum *(see p63)* on Red Square.

Top 10 Cultural Events

1 Biennale of Contemporary Art (Feb)
Month-long contemporary art festival at various city venues. ☏ http://3rd.moscowbiennale.ru

2 Golden Mask Festival (Feb/Mar)
A month of drama, opera, ballet, music and puppet shows. ☏ www.goldenmask.ru

3 Moscow Forum (Apr)
A week of 20th-century classical music concerts and workshops. ☏ www.ccmm.ru

4 Boheme Jazz Festival (May)
Jazz festival held in late May. ☏ *International House of Music: Map G5; Kosmodamianskaya nab 52/8, Zamoskvoreche; 730 1011*

5 Moscow Stars Festival (May)
A week of classical concerts organized by the Moscow State Philharmonic Society. ☏ http://classicalmusic.ru

6 Moscow International Film Festival (Jun)
Moscow's cinemas screen Russian and international films. ☏ www.moscowfilmfestival.ru

7 Russian Fashion Week (Apr and Oct)
Twice a year Russia's top new designers show their work. ☏ http://russianfashionweek.com

8 International Folk Music Festival (Oct)
An event hosted at the Central House of Artists *(see p38)*.

9 Jazz Voices (Dec)
Performances by Russian and international jazz vocalists.

10 December Evenings Festival (Dec)
Classical concerts held at the Pushkin Museum of Fine Arts *(see pp16–17)*.

Left **Gostiny Dvor mall** Right **Shoppers on Ulitsa Arbat**

🔟 Shops and Markets

1 Manezh Mall
Built three storeys under-ground next to the Alexander Gardens in the 1990s, this smart mall is packed with mainstream clothes shops and an entire floor of eateries *(see p86)*.

2 Dorogomilovsky Market
The vast Dorogomilovsky food market is lined with tidy kiosks manned by uniformed traders, with polite porters on hand to carry heavy bags. Live fish and lobsters, endless rows of olives, neatly stacked vegetables, sauces, spices and cheeses are among the astonishing variety of produce from Russia and beyond.
🅜 *Map B4 • Ulitsa Mozhayskiy val 10 • Metro: Kievskaya • Open 7am–8pm*

3 Izmaylovo Market
Best visited at weekends, Izmaylovo Market has a bewildering number of stalls selling everything from carpets and household goods to books, clothes and souvenirs. Look out for *matryoshka* dolls and Soviet memorabilia, both in plentiful supply. Shoppers will need to haggle to find a bargain here.
🅜 *Map B1 • 3 Ulitsa Parkovaya 24 • Metro: Partizanskaya • Open 8am–8pm*

4 Ulitsa Arbat
The Arbat was once the hub of Moscow's intelligentsia. Today the pedestrianized street attracts tourists and locals looking for souvenirs, jewellery, and antiques as well as patronizing its restaurants and bars *(see p74)*.

5 Ulitsa Petrovka
Once home to Moscow's aristocratic elite, the majestic 19th-century buildings of Ulitsa Petrovka have long since been taken over by high-class shops and smart restaurants. Opposite the Marriott Tverskaya *(see p117)* hotel stands the upmarket Petrovskiy Pasazh. This gleaming marble-floored mall, built in 1903, is today the city's premier shop-ping strip *(see p86)*.

6 Ulitsa Tverskaya
Historically significant as the road that led from the Kremlin to the once-powerful city of Tver and beyond,

Izmaylovo Market in winter

 Preceding pages **Elegant Novodevichiy Convent**

to St Petersburg, Ulitsa Tverskaya was straightened and widened during the Soviet era and is now lined with shops, restaurants, museums and theatres (see p86).

House of Foreign Books

Opened in 1936, this lovely bookshop retains its original wooden floor-to-ceiling shelves, which are filled with over 20,000 foreign-language titles. Most are in English and include everything from novels to academic texts, TEFL reference material and guide books. ◎ Map N2 • Kuznetskiy Most 18/7 • Metro: Kuznetskiy Most • Open 9am–9pm Mon–Fri, 10am–9pm Sat, 10am–8pm Sun

The well-stocked House of Foreign Books

TsUM

Founded by a pair of Scottish entrepreneurs in 1857, TsUM was known as Myur and Meriliz until it was nationalized by the Communists. The imposing seven-storey building dates back to 1908 and is now occupied by high-end shops stocking designer labels (see p86).

GUM

One of Moscow's must-see landmarks, GUM is a wonderful 19th-century shopping

The 19th-century GUM shopping mall

mall consisting of three capacious parallel halls covered by a glass roof and filled with boutiques, cafés and ice-cream parlours (see p64).

Gostiny Dvor

There has been a market on the site of Gostiny Dvor since the 16th century. Various trading structures have stood here since then, and the current building was completed in 1830. It consists of three floors of shops and cafés overlooking a spacious courtyard. A glass roof was added in 1995. ◎ Map N3 • Ulitsa Ilinka 4 • Metro: Ploshchad Revolyutsii, Kitay Gorod

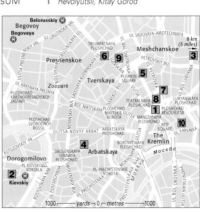

Left **Sea Aquarium** Centre **Yuri Nikulin's Old Moscow Circus** Right **Moscow Cats Theatre**

🔟 Children's Attractions

1 Arlekino Children's Club

This popular club offers an excellent range of activities, from supervised play areas and a trampoline to singing and dancing classes. Drinks are included in the ticket price. ✎ *Map G4 • Ulitsa Verkhnaya Radishchevskaya 19/3 • (495) 915 1106 • Metro: Taganskaya • Open 1–10pm Mon–Fri, noon–10pm Sat–Sun • Adm*

2 Moscow Puppet Theatre

The puppet shows here are aimed at children, but there are also absurdist and experimental performances for adults. The shows usually involve actors, who operate the puppets and participate brilliantly as characters in the story. ✎ *Map H2 • Ulitsa Spartakovskaya 26/30 • (495) 267 4288 • Metro: Baumanskaya • Open 11am–6pm Tue–Sun • Adm*

Sign, Arlekino Children's Club

3 Obraztsov Puppet Theatre

Named after master puppeteer Sergey Obraztsov (1901–92), who was the director here for 60 years, Russia's largest puppet theatre stages entertaining shows that appeal to both children and adults. It also features a museum of more than 3,000 puppets. ✎ *Map E1 • Ulitsa Sadoyova-Samotyochnaya 3 • (495) 699 5373 • Metro: Tsvetnoy Bulvar • Shows at 11am, 2pm, 5pm • Adm • www.puppet.ru*

4 Moscow Zoo

Covering a huge site, Moscow Zoo is home to more than 960 species. There are regular feeding shows and introductions to some of its 5,000 inhabitants. ✎ *Map J2 • Ulitsa Bolshaya Gruzinskaya 1 • (495) 255 6034 • Metro: Krasnopresnenskaya • Apr–Sep: 10am–8pm Tue–Sun; Oct–Mar: 10am–5pm Tue–Sun • Adm*

5 Sea Aquarium

More of a vast exotic fish shop than a public aquarium, the Sea Aquarium makes for a fascinating visit. ✎ *Map Q2 • Chistoprudny Bulvar 14 • (495) 623 2261 • Metro: Chistye Prudy • Open 10am–7pm Mon–Fri, 10am–6pm Sat–Sun • Adm*

Puppet show at the Obraztsov Puppet Theatre

The Moscow Ocean Centre, which will feature three underwater tanks, is scheduled to open in Victory Park (see p45) in 2011.

Gorky Park

This delightful riverside park has play areas, funfairs, a ferris wheel with fantastic views and an original Russian Buran space shuttle (see p90).

7 Durov Animal Theatre

Vladimir Durov created this unique theatre in 1912 when he started training

A performance at the Children's Musical Theatre

exotic animals, such as sea lions and anteaters, to perform tricks. The theatre now has a large main stage and a smaller stage aimed at younger children. Acts include waltzing horses, dancing porcupines and a smiling hippo. ☏ Map F1 • Ulitsa Durova 4 • (495) 631 3029 • Metro: Prospekt Mira • Large stage: shows at noon, 3pm, 6pm Thu–Sun; small stage: shows at 11am, 2pm Wed–Sun • Adm

8 Moscow Cats Theatre

The stars of this surreal theatre are 120 cats trained by clown Yuri Kuklachev to perform simple tricks alongside actors. The cats also feature in shows such as Cats from Outer Space and a rough adaptation of The Nutcracker. ☏ Map B4 • Kutuzovskiy Prospekt 25 • (499) 249 2907 • Metro: Kutuzovo • Open 11am–6pm (ticket office); shows at 4pm, 6pm Wed–Fri; 3pm, 7pm Sat–Sun • Adm • www.catstheatre.ru

9 Children's Musical Theatre

This theatre was opened in 1965 by Natalia Sats, who aimed to bring opera, ballet and musicals to

a younger audience. She adapted works such as Madame Butterfly and Evgeni Onegin. ☏ Map A3 • Vernadskovo Prospekt 5 • (495) 930 7021 • Metro: Universitet • Open noon–6pm (ticket office) • Adm • http://teatr-sats.ru

10 Yuri Nikulin's Old Moscow Circus

Moscow's first permanent circus was established in 1880 and it has continued to function ever since, with a hugely entertaining repertoire featuring animals, acrobats and magicians. Legendary clown Yuri Nikulin was director from 1982 to 1997. ☏ Map F2 • Tsvetnoy Bulvar 13 • (495) 625 8970 • Metro: Tsvetnoy Bulvar • Shows at 2:30pm, 6pm • Adm • www.circusnikulin.ru

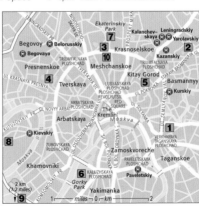

In winter, frozen footpaths transform Gorky Park into a giant skating rink and ice sculptors fill the park with their creations.

55

Left **Band performing at B2, Moscow's biggest nightclub** Right **Exterior of Bilingua**

🔟 Bars and Clubs

1 Karma
Extremely popular with Muscovites, Karma has a great atmosphere and vaguely oriental styling. The bar puts on regular salsa events as well as karaoke, disco, and live gigs. Steamy bar-top strippers are on hand when things get lively. ✆ Map N2
• Ulitsa Pushechnaya 3 • (495) 924 5633
• Metro: Kuznetskiy Most • Open 9pm–6am Wed–Sun • Adm

2 Bilingua
Festooned with bizarre art works, this cosily cluttered club hosts wacky underground performances and concerts, and serves cheap drinks and meals.
✆ Map P2 • Krivokolenniy pereulok 10/5
• (495) 623 9660 • Metro: Turgenskaya
• Open 24 hrs • Adm

3 Ikra
At Ikra, embossed wallpaper, gilt-framed mirrors and plush furnishings contribute to a chic saturnine style that attracts an urbane crowd. The club also boasts a great sound system and is large enough to host international guests, such as Coldcut and Gogol Bordello.
✆ Map H3 • Ulitsa Kazakova 8a • (495) 778 5651 • Metro: Kurskaya • Open noon–6am • Adm

4 Propaganda
This legendary club, which is frequented by expatriates and Moscow's art professionals, is one of the city's coolest spots. Literally anything goes: music ranges from retro and rock to electronica and there is a gay night every Sunday. The dance floor transforms into a popular restaurant by day. ✆ Map P2
• Bolshoy Zlatoustinskiy pereulok 7
• (495) 624 5737 • Metro: Lubyanka
• Open noon–6am

5 Denis Simachev
Patronized by Moscow's attractive young socialites, who flaunt their wealth in perpetual party mode, this wildly extravagant club is located on the ground floor of the exclusive Denis Simachev menswear boutique. Bouncers ensure that standards remain high. ✆ Map M1
• Stoleshnikov pereulok 12/2 • (495) 629 8085
• Metro: Pushkinskaya
• Open 24 hrs • Adm

The bar at Ikra

Bilingua organizes music and art workshops most weekends, as well as screening children's films.

16 Tons

6 This kitsch reproduction of a classic English pub has its own real ale brewery and a great menu that includes Russian favourites as well as bacon and eggs. Upstairs is a spacious club hosting frequent live gigs and DJs. ◎ Map C2 • Ulitsa Presnenskiy val 6/1 • (495) 253 5300 • Metro: Ulitsa 1905 Goda • Open 11am–6am

Zona

7 This funky dance club can accommodate up to 3,000 people over its five floors. The main dance area caters to techno lovers, while a stylish lower floor with fluffy wall coverings plays R&B. The upper levels are reserved for VIPs. ◎ Map B2 • Ulitsa Leninskaya Sloboda 19/2 • (495) 229 1428 • Metro: Avtozavodskaya • Open 11pm–8am Fri–Sun • Adm

Gaudi Arena

8 The city's largest dance floor can accommodate up to 6,000 clubbers. State-of-the-art sound and light systems, club nights run by the UK's Gatecrasher, and famous guest DJs make this place a magnet for hardcore house and techno fans. ◎ Map A1 • Ulitsa Skladochnaya 1 • (495) 508 8060 • Metro: Savelovskaya • Open 8pm–6am • Adm

The unassuming exterior of Gogol

Gogol

9 Attracting a bohemian crowd, Gogol is one of Moscow's best venues for the latest underground sounds. It stages regular live gigs by lesser-known Russian and international groups, featuring everything from pop-punk to avant-garde. ◎ Map M1 • Stoleshnikov pereulok 11 • (495) 514 0944 • Metro: Teatralnaya • Open 9pm–6am • Adm

B2

10 Moscow's largest club covers five floors arranged around a huge concert hall with frequent live bands and DJs. Facilities include a pub, restaurant, jazz club, chill-out level and a VIP area for the city's elite. ◎ Map D2 • Ulitsa Bolshaya Sadovaya 8/1 • (495) 650 9918 • Metro: Mayakovskaya • Open noon–6am • Adm

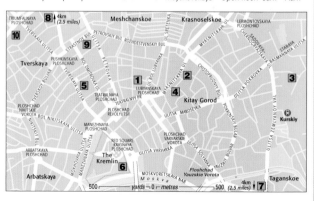

Left **The Savoy dining room** Right **Sign outside Tiflis**

Restaurants

Savoy
The Savoy restaurant is as richly decorated today as it was upon opening in 1913. Its opulent Rococo main hall features gilt and marble, as well as plush chairs. The menu covers both Russian and international cuisine *(see p73)*.

Tiflis
This is one of the best spots in Moscow to sample Georgian cuisine, a Russian favourite. The lovely outdoor dining area is shaded by trees and vines. The *shashlik* (skewers of fish, pork, lamb and beef) served here is excellent *(see p79)*.

Café Pushkin
The epitome of high-class Moscow, Café Pushkin is evocative of 19th-century Russian society, with liveried waiters, antique furnishings and international cuisine fit for a tsar. The Stone Hall is perhaps the most elegant of the themed rooms here, while the sophisticated Library has great views of Tverskoy Bulvar *(see p87)*.

Red Square
Located within the Historical Museum *(see p63)*, this fine restaurant specializes in reproducing recipes once served to royalty. The menu incorporates anecdotal descriptions of dishes, such as *solianka* (a spicy meat soup), which dates back to the 10th century *(see p67)*.

Uzbekistan
This restaurant is one of Moscow's oldest, dating from 1951. Its carved wooden doors lead into an opulent interior of oriental carpets and chandeliers. Belly dancers offer entertainment, peacocks strut about in

Elegant antique furnishings, Café Pushkin

From September to May, Red Square hosts "Historical Dinners," in which 12-course ceremonial feasts from the past are re-created.

the fairytale summer garden and cockfights take place on Monday nights *(see p73)*.

Yoko
By flying in fresh fish from Tokyo twice a week and employing an award-winning sushi chef, Yoko has carved out an exclusive niche of its own among Moscow's countless Japanese eateries. It also has superb views of the Cathedral of Christ the Saviour *(see p75)*. ◎ *Map L5 • 5 Soymonovskiy proezd • (495) 290 1217 • Metro: Kropotkinskaya • RRRR*

Oblomov
Housed in a grand old mansion refurbished in 19th-century imperial style, Oblomov serves up traditional Russian dishes, accompanied by an impressive wine list. Diners can relax with hookah pipes in a Middle Eastern-style attic area and there is also a pleasant outdoor terrace *(see p93)*.

Dorian Gray
Highly regarded for the consistent quality of its cuisine, Dorian Gray is popular with the city's elite. Rumour has it that this is one of Vladimir Putin's favourite restaurants. The Sicilian chef's tiramisu is legendary *(see p93)*.

Artists' Gallery
This restaurant is testament to the phenomenal artistic output of its owner, Zurab Tsereteli *(see p76)*, whose canvases adorn the walls of several themed dining rooms. The cuisine is a blend of European and

Colourful interior, Artists' Gallery restaurant

Japanese, with an emphasis on creative presentation. ◎ *Map K6 • Ulitsa Prechistenka 19 • (495) 637 3522 • Metro: Kropotkinskaya • RRRRR*

Noev Kovcheg
Moscow's top Armenian restaurant offers a rare experience of the country's cuisine and culture. Fresh fish and meat are flown in from Armenia to prepare authentic dishes, Armenian cognacs are in plentiful supply and live music is performed by traditional folk groups *(see p73)*.

AROUND TOWN

MOSCOW'S TOP 10

A view of the Kremlin from across the Moskva river

The Kremlin and Red Square

MOSCOW'S HISTORIC CENTRE *is the obvious starting point for tours of this ancient city, which started life as a 12th-century citadel enclosed by wooden walls. Today the Kremlin, with its magnificent ensemble of palaces and cathedrals, is home to the Russian president. Despite limited public access, it leaves a powerful impression of the country's colourful past. Neighbouring Red Square, long used for public ceremonies and parades, continues to be a focal point of city life, adorned with the iconic domes of St Basil's Cathedral.*

Left **Historical Museum at Red Square** Right **Magnificent interior of the Great Kremlin Palace**

🔟 Sights

1 St Basil's Cathedral
2 Lenin Mausoleum
3 Historical Museum
4 Kremlin Wall Graves
5 State Armoury
6 GUM
7 Great Kremlin Palace
8 Cathedral of the Assumption
9 Faceted Palace
10 Patriarch's Palace

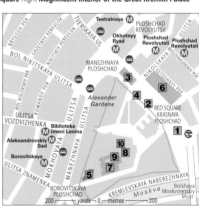

Preceding pages **Interior of the GUM shopping mall**

The jewel-like domes of St Basil's Cathedral

Historical Museum

Founded in 1872, this museum has amassed an incredible collection of over 4.5 million objects, of which around 22,000 are on permanent display. The exhibition begins with traces of early Palaeolithic man and goes on to chart Russian history through the ages. Its neatly arranged displays of fascinating artifacts include a 7.5-m (24.5-ft) Neolithic dug-out canoe, a massive marble sarcophagus from the 4th century BC and a large wooden globe produced by Dutch cartographers and acquired by Peter the Great in 1697. ◈ *Map M3 • Krasnaya Ploshchad 1 • (495) 692 4019 • Metro: Okhotnyy Ryad, Ploshchad Revolyutsii • Open 10am–6pm Mon–Sat, 11am–8pm Sun • Adm • www.shm.ru*

St Basil's Cathedral

Moscow's most fanciful landmark was built in the 16th century to mark the conquest of Kazan, which effectively ended centuries of Mongolian Tatar rule in Russia. Combining motifs from Kazan's mosque with elements of Russian Orthodox style, the cathedral's design is a triumphant fusion of East and West, symbolic of Russia's victory *(see pp8–9)*.

Lenin Mausoleum

The imposing granite mausoleum was designed by the acclaimed Russian architect Aleksey Shchusev in 1930. Visitors are not permitted to linger beside the crystal casket containing Lenin's embalmed body, prompting rumours that it is a wax replica, but the authorities insist that a special chemical formula developed by Soviet scientists has preserved him to this day. ◈ *Map N3 • Krasnaya Ploshchad • Metro: Okhotnyy Ryad, Ploshchad Revolyutsii • Open 10am–1pm Tue–Thu, Sat–Sun*

Kremlin Wall Graves

The section of Kremlin wall behind Lenin's mausoleum was first used as a necropolis in 1917 when the bodies of 238 Bolshevik revolutionary fighters were buried in mass graves there. Since then over 100 Soviet heroes have had their ashes interred in the wall and marked with plaques. Twelve Soviet statesmen, including every leader except Khrushchev, are honoured with individual tombs. ◈ *Map M3 • Krasnaya Ploshchad • Metro: Biblioteka im. Lenina, Okhotnyy Ryad*

Tomb of the Unknown Soldier, Kremlin Wall Graves

Festival of Torture

Some of Ivan the Terrible's worst excesses took place publicly in Red Square on 25 June 1570 during what was to become known as the Festival of Torture. Ivan spent the day "entertaining" onlookers by torturing 180 prisoners convicted of conspiring against him, employing hot pincers, ropes tautened so as to splice bodies in half, and a human-sized frying pan.

State Armoury

The Armoury's stunning collection is housed in a grand building that was designed in 1844 by Konstantin Ton (1794–1881). Besides ornately decorated armoury from Russia, Europe and the Far East, the museum exhibits precious items once coveted by Russia's ruling classes *(see pp14–15)*.

"Summer Carriage", State Armoury

GUM

One of Moscow's major landmarks, GUM (State Department Store) was built in the late 19th century on a site where market stalls had existed since the 15th century. It consists of three parallel halls faced with polished marble and covered with a glass roof designed by engineering genius Vladimir Shukhov (1853–1939). The mall is now privately owned and has around 200 high-end boutiques, cafés and food stores. ⊗ *Map N3 • Krasnaya Ploshchad • Metro: Ploshchad Revolyutsii • Open 10am–10pm*

Great Kremlin Palace

The Kremlin's largest building was built by Konstantin Tor for Tsar Nicholas I between 1838 and 1849 on the site of an older palace. Today it is the official residence of the president. Though rarely open to the public, parts of its interior are often seen on TV as the setting for official ceremonies and international meetings. ⊗ *Map M4 • Kremlin • Metro: Biblioteka im. Lenina, Borovitskaya • www.kreml.ru*

Cathedral of the Assumption

The cathedral's sturdy yet graceful design is the result of Italian architect Aristotle Fioravanti's skilful fusion of Russian Orthodox

Grand marble interior of the GUM shopping centre

Cathedral of the Assumption, Kremlin

features with Renaissance motifs. The interior has glorious gilt frescoes and is dominated by a huge iconostasis containing numerous precious icons *(see pp12–13)*.

Faceted Palace

Off limits to the public today, this palace was built by Italian architects in the 15th century and owes its name to its Renaissance-style faceted stone façade. An external staircase leads up to a richly painted chamber that occupies the entire upper floor. This was once the royal throne room, but in recent years it has been used as a banquet hall for visiting dignitaries. ⊗ *Map M4 • Kremlin • Metro: Biblioteka im. Lenina, Borovitskaya • Adm • www.kreml.ru*

Patriarch's Palace

Built for Patriarch Nikon (1605–81) in the 17th century to replace the previous patriarch's humbler residential quarters, the palace was decorated with murals and connected to the patriarch's private Twelve Apostles' Church. Its finest room is the Cross Chamber, which was used as a reception hall. Today the room displays precious artworks, bound bibles, churchware and ecclesiastical robes. ⊗ *Map M4 • Kremlin • Metro: Biblioteka im. Lenina, Borovitskaya • Open 10am–5pm • Adm • www.kreml.ru*

A Tour Around the Heart of Moscow

Morning

Start at Okhotnyy Ryad metro station and walk towards the Kremlin, passing **Kilometre Zero** *(see p11)* and pausing to admire the tiny Iverskaya Chapel where royal visitors used to pray before passing through **Resurrection Gate** *(see p11)* and into **Red Square**. Just to the right is the **Historical Museum** *(see p63)*, while to the left is **Kazan Cathedral** *(see p37)*. Leave bags and cameras in the Historical Museum's cloakroom before joining the queue for the **Lenin Mausoleum** *(see p63)* and **Kremlin Wall Graves** *(see p63)*. Walk south towards **St Basil's Cathedral** *(see p63)* before entering the narrow passages linking its chapels, pausing to admire its symmetry from its western side. For a light lunch try **Bosco Café** *(see p67)*.

Afternoon

Exit Red Square via Resurrection Gate and turn left past the **Statue of Marshal Zhukov** *(see p10)* and into **Alexander Gardens** *(see p66)* beneath the Kremlin wall. Keep walking until you reach the causeway connecting the Kremlin to Kutafya Tower, where tickets for the **State Armoury** *(see pp14–15)* and Kremlin buildings are sold separately. Visit the State Armoury, where tickets are sold for the **Diamond Fund** *(see p15)*. For a budget dinner head for the **Manezh Mall Food Court** *(see p67)*, or return to the Historical Museum for a superb meal at the **Red Square** restaurant *(see p67)*.

Left **Tsar Cannon** Centre **Alexander Gardens** Right **Church of the Deposition of the Robe**

🔟 Best of the Rest

1 Terem Palace
This three-floor tower was used as the imperial residence from 1635 until 1712, when the capital moved to St Petersburg. Its lovely stained-glass windows and murals were restored in the 19th century. 🕾 *Map M4*

2 State Kremlin Palace
The State Kremlin Palace contains 800 rooms and a huge conference hall. Much of the structure is concealed 15 m (49 ft) underground *(see p41)*.

3 Cathedral of the Archangel
Chosen to house the royal necropolis, this wonderfully frescoed cathedral contains the tombs of the 54 princes and tsars who died between 1340 and 1730. 🕾 *Map M4 • Adm*

4 Tsar Cannon
Originally positioned on Red Square as a symbol of Russian power, this enormous bronze cannon was cast in 1586 and weighs 39,000 kg (43 tons).

5 Tsar Bell
At 199,580 kg (220 tons), this is the world's largest bell. A 10,890-kg (12-ton) chunk broke off after casting in 1735, and the bell remained unused until it was displayed here in 1835.

6 Ivan the Great Bell Tower
Once the tallest building in Moscow, the 81-m (266-ft) bell tower was built in the 16th century. It contains 20 bells on two levels and was also used as a watchtower. 🕾 *Map M4*

7 Cathedral of the Annunciation
Built in the 15th century, this church has superb interior frescoes, including a portrait of Christ by Simon Ushakov. 🕾 *Map M4*

8 Church of the Deposition of the Robe
This 15th-century church was built for private use by metropolitans and patriarchs *(see p12)*. Inside is an exhibition of medieval wooden sculptures. 🕾 *Map M4*

9 Saviour's Tower
The Kremlin's largest tower rises to a height of 70 m (230 ft). Built in 1491, it was enlarged in 1625, with the addition of its first chiming clock. 🕾 *Map N3*

10 Alexander Gardens
These gardens were created in 1812 after the Neglinnaya river was channelled underground. The Memorial of the Unknown Soldier is situated here. 🕾 *Map M3*

The State Kremlin Palace is open to the public for occasional concerts and events (see p41).

Price Categories

For a three-course meal for one with half a bottle of house wine (or equivalent meal).

R	Under 800 Rub
RR	800–1,500 Rub
RRR	1,500–2,000 Rub
RRRR	2,000–2,500 Rub
RRRRR	Over 2,500 Rub

Boutiques inside the GUM shopping mall

Shops, Cafés and Restaurants

1 Red Square
This high-class restaurant specializes in dishes that were once prepared for royalty *(see p58)*. ✎ *Map M3 • Historical Museum • Krasnaya Ploshchad 1 • (495) 692 1196 • Metro: Okhotnyy Ryad • RRRRR*

2 Drova Café
Ambient lighting, laid-back music and polite staff add to Drova Café's appeal. ✎ *Map M3 • Ulitsa Nikolskaya 5 • (495) 698 2484 • Metro: Okhotnyy Ryad • RR*

3 Historical Museum Gift Shop
All manner of Russian souvenirs, from wolf skins to stuffed bears, can be found at this gift shop. ✎ *Map M3 • Krasnaya Ploshchad 1 • Metro: Okhotnyy Ryad*

4 GUM
A 19th-century shopping mall, GUM offers a range of designer boutiques and cafés *(see p64)*. ✎ *Map N3 • Krasnaya Ploshchad • Metro: Ploshchad Revolyutsii*

5 Bosco Café
Bosco, a retro-style café, draws a fashionable crowd. Sample fancy ice cream and cakes while enjoying the view of Red Square. ✎ *Map N3 • GUM • (495) 620 3182 • Metro: Ploshchad Revolyutsii*

6 Planet Sushi
Located opposite Alexander Gardens, Planet Sushi is part of a hugely popular sushi chain that has efficient staff and good standards. ✎ *Map M3 • Manezhnaya 1/2 • (495) 730 2251 • Metro: Biblioteka im. Lenina • RR*

7 Market Stalls
Occupying the cobbled street in front of Resurrection Gate are many souvenir stalls selling cheap Soviet memorabilia. ✎ *Map M3 • Krasnaya Ploshchad • Metro: Okhotnyy Ryad*

8 Manezh Mall Food Court
The ground floor of this underground mall is packed with inexpensive eateries. ✎ *Map M3 • Manezhnaya Ploshchad • Metro: Okhotnyy Ryad*

9 Krushka Pub
This fantastic cellar pub has several dimly lit halls popular with beer-swigging students. ✎ *Map N2 • Ulitsa Nikolskaya 15 • (495) 710 7199 • Metro: Ploshchad Revolyutsii • R*

10 Café Norma
Featuring bare brick walls, this funky café transforms into a vibrant club at night. ✎ *Map N3 • Ulitsa Nikolskaya 4/5 • (495) 698 3809 • Metro: Ploshchad Revolyutsii • RR*

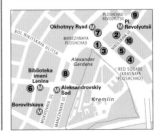

Left **Entrance to the Mayakovsky Museum** Right **Official Chamber, Old English Court**

Kitay Gorod

MOSCOW'S EARLIEST RESIDENTIAL *and trading quarter, Kitay Gorod continues to be a thriving commercial centre and is home to numerous bars and clubs. Its main shopping streets, Nikolskaya and Ilinka, are packed with malls and restaurants. Despite the demolition of large parts of the area during the Soviet era, it still has some notable historic buildings, many of which can be found along Ulitsa Varvarka. The area now stretches beyond its original boundaries to encompass the pleasant gardens and ponds of Chistye Prudy.*

A view along Ulitsa Varvarka

🔟 Sights

1. Church of the Trinity in Nikitniki
2. Ulitsa Varvarka
3. Mayakovsky Museum
4. Epiphany Cathedral
5. Moscow City Museum
6. Old English Court
7. Archaeological Museum
8. Choral Synagogue
9. Palace of the Romanov Boyars
10. Polytechnical Museum

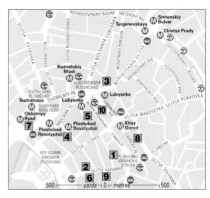

Kitay Gorod was once protected by stone walls, remnants of which lie behind the Metropol hotel on Teatralnyy proezd.

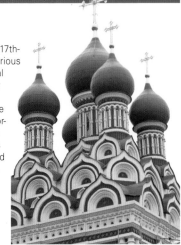

1 Church of the Trinity in Nikitniki

A fine example of Moscow's 17th-century architecture, this glorious church was endowed by local nobleman Grigoriy Nikitnikov and built on his estate from 1634 to 1654. Its modest size is compensated by the elaborate exterior decoration, with its five onion-domed cupolas perched above tiers of arched niches known as *kokoshniki*. During Communism the church was turned into a museum, but the interior has now been restored and the bold frescoes, by Simon Ushakov, are once again in pristine condition.

The 17th-century Church of the Trinity in Nikitniki

Ⓢ Map P3 • Nikitnikov pereulok 3 • Metro: Kitay Gorod • Open 10am–5pm • www.nikitniki.ru/eng

2 Ulitsa Varvarka

Counted amongst Moscow's oldest streets, Ulitsa Varvarka is named after St Varvara Church, one of several along its length. The street and its churches are almost all that remain of historic Zaryadye, a bustling quarter of artisans and traders that was flattened by Soviet city planners. Under Communism, all the churches were closed and transformed into museums, concert halls, or residential quarters. Ⓢ Map N3 • Metro: Kitay Gorod

3 Mayakovsky Museum

Vladimir Mayakovsky (1893–1930) was one of Russia's leading Futurist artists and poets. Inspired by the October Revolution of 1917, he developed a style that he named Communist Futurism, and for a time produced propaganda posters and poetry, which earned him official approval. However, by his mid-30s, Mayakovsky had become disillusioned with his two great passions – love and Communism – and on 14 April 1930 he shot himself. The museum celebrates his life with sculptures, photographs, poetry, pictures and posters. Ⓢ Map P2 • Lubyanskiy Prospekt 3/6 • (495) 621 9560 • Metro: Lubyanka • Open 1–9pm Thu, 10am–6pm Fri–Tue • Adm • www.museum.ru/majakovskiy

4 Epiphany Cathedral

This cathedral, replete with intricate white stone ornamentation, was completed in 1696. It belonged to one of Moscow's oldest monasteries and was originally surrounded by monks' cells and an abbot's residence. The monastery was founded in the 13th century and thrived for several centuries under the patronage of successive tsars, but was closed by the Communists, who used it to accommodate labourers building the city's metro system. The cathedral was re-opened for religious services in 1991. Ⓢ Map N3 • Bogoyavlevskiy pereulok • Metro: Ploshchad Revolyutsii • Open 10am–7pm

Ex-Rossiya Hotel

The great space beyond Ulitsa Varvarka, which once comprised the Zaryadye district, was originally created over 50 years ago to make way for Stalin's eighth skyscraper *(see p46)*, a project that never took shape. The site lay empty until the 1960s when it was filled by one of the Soviet era's ugliest buildings: the 3,000-room Hotel Rossiya, which was demolished in 2007.

Moscow City Museum

This museum was housed in the 17th-century Sukharov Tower until the Communists destroyed the building in 1934. The collection of photographs, ancient maps, antique jewellery and other exhibits was then transferred to its current location – a 19th-century church that had been closed by the atheistic government. *Map N2 • Novaya Ploshchad 12 • (495) 624 8490 • Metro: Lubyanka • Open 10am–6pm Tue, Thu–Sat; 11am–7pm Wed, Sun • Adm • www.mosmuseum.ru*

Old English Court

In 1553, English merchants seeking a northern sea passage to China got as far as Murmansk, from where they sledged 2,000 km (1,240 miles) to Moscow. Impressed by their bravery and keen to establish trade relations with the West, Ivan the Terrible granted them trade rights and the use of what became known as the Old English Court. The museum offers a glimpse into historic diplomatic relations between England and Russia. *Map N3 • Ulitsa Varvarka 4a • (495) 698 3952 • Metro: Kitay Gorod • Open 10am–6pm Tue, Thu, Sat–Sun; 11am–7pm Wed, Fri • Adm • www.mosmuseum.ru*

Archaeological Museum

Entered via a glass-roofed archway opposite Resurrection Gate, this subterranean museum is based around the foundations of the 16th-century Voskresenky Bridge. Displays include ceramic tiles and silver coins unearthed during excavations. *Map M3 • Manezhnaya Ploshchad 1a • (495) 692 4147 • Metro: Teatralnaya • Open 10am–6pm Tue–Sun • Adm • www.mosmuseum.ru*

Choral Synagogue

Largely funded by banker Lazar Polyakov, the construction of this splendid synagogue began in 1887, but was abandoned after Moscow's governor ordered the expulsion of all but 5,000 Jews in 1891. It was not completed until 1906. With a lovely Moorish-style interior, the synagogue draws the city's growing Jewish community. *Map P3 • Bolshoy Spasoglinishchevskiy pereulok 10 • Metro: Kitay Gorod • Open 10am–6pm Mon–Fri*

Elegant façade of the Choral Synagogue

Interior, Palace of the Romanov Boyars

9 Palace of the Romanov Boyars

This palace was home to the Romanov family before they moved into the Kremlin after Michael (1596–1645) became the first Romanov tsar in 1613. It was then neglected until the 1850s when Nicholas I (1796–1855) had it restored and opened as a museum. The splendidly furnished men's quarters are on the ground floor; the women would weave and embroider in the rooms upstairs. ◈ Map N3 • Ulitsa Varvarka 10 • (495) 298 3706 • Metro: Kitay Gorod • Open 11am–7pm Wed, 10am–6pm Thu–Mon • Adm

10 Polytechnical Museum

This is one of Moscow's most engaging museums, with a fascinating array of exhibits displayed over four vast floors in an imposing 19th-century building. The basement has a fine collection of antique cars, bicycles and motorbikes, including a Penny Farthing and a rare 1915 Triumph N motorbike, while the upper floors are occupied by themed exhibitions. ◈ Map N2 • Novaya Ploshchad 3/4 • (495) 624 7356 • Metro: Lubyanka • Open 10am–6pm Tue, Thu, Sat–Sun; 11am–7pm Wed, Fri • Adm • www.polymus.ru

A Day in Kitay Gorod

Morning

Arriving at Kitay Gorod metro station, follow exit signs for Slavyanskiy Ploshchad. Once outside, head for the small green domes of **Church of St George** on the left side of **Ulitsa Varvarka** (see p69). From here cross over to Ipatevskiy pereulok and turn right for the stunning **Church of the Trinity in Nikitniki** (see p69) on Nikitnikov pereulok. Retrace your steps to St George's Church and continue west following signs to the **Palace of the Romanov Boyars** for a glimpse of medieval aristocratic life. Continue to the **Old English Court** before emerging onto Red Square at the end of Ulitsa Varvarka. Opposite stands the grand **Gostiny Dvor** shopping mall (see p53), where the Amsterdam Café makes a great spot for lunch.

Afternoon

From Gostiny Dvor head east away from the Kremlin along Ulitsa Ilinka and turn left onto Novaya Ploshchad, where you can visit the vast **Polytechnical Museum**, or the smaller **Moscow City Museum** opposite. Head up the street towards Lubyanka Ploshchad, home to the infamous ex-KGB head-quarters. The **Mayakovsky Museum** (see p69) is on nearby Lubyanskiy proezd. The well-stocked **Biblio Globus** bookshop stands on adjoining Ulitsa Mayasnitskaya. For dinner you can either try **GlavPivTorg** (see p73) on the corner of Ulitsa Bolshaya Lubyanka, or splash out at the chic **Dissident** (see p73).

At the Polytechnical Museum, look out for the "radiogramophone" presented to Stalin by Latvian workers in 1950.

Left **Ludi Kak Ludi** Centre **Sign, Jao-Da** Right **An outdoor café, Kitay Gorod**

🔟 Cafés and Bars

1 Coffee House
An American-style café, the Coffee House serves coffee, cakes and snacks. ❧ Map N3 • Ulitsa Ilinka 13/19 str. 2 • (495) 221 8381 • Metro: Ploshchad Revolyutsii • Open 24 hrs

2 Discreet Charm of the Bourgeoisie
This funky bar serves affordable food and plays noisy disco beats at weekends. ❧ Map P1 • Ulitsa Bolshaya Lubyanka 24 • (495) 623 0848 • Metro: Lubyanka • Open 24 hrs

3 Ludi Kak Ludi
Small café featuring Russian *pirogi* (dumplings) and a variety of juices and cocktails. ❧ Map P3 • Solyanski Tupik 1/4 • Metro: Kitay Gorod • Open 8am–11pm Mon–Wed, Sun; 8am–3am Thu; 8am–6am Fri; 11am–6am Sat

4 Vogue Café
A stylish café with a modern European menu, Vogue attracts a fashionable crowd. ❧ Map M2 • Kuznetskiy Most 7/9 • (495) 623 1701 • Metro: Kuznetskiy Most • Open 24 hrs

5 Che
More bar-cum-club than café, Che plays Latin music, drawing a boisterous crowd. ❧ Map N2 • Ulitsa Nikolosyaka 10/2 • (495) 621 7477 • Metro: Lubyanka • Open 24 hrs

6 Shokoladnitsa
Part of a chain, this café serves savoury and fresh fruit pancakes along with cakes. ❧ Map P2 • Ulitsa Maroseyka 3 • (495) 624 0779 • Metro: Kitay Gorod • Open 24 hrs

7 Jagannath
The café at Jagannath offers tea and superb Indian vegetarian food. ❧ Map N2 • Kuznetskiy Most 11 • (495) 628 3580 • Metro: Kuznetskiy Most • Open 10am–11pm

8 Lilienthal
A very stylish bar, Lilienthal attracts an equally stylish crowd. The bottled Russian cider is highly recommended. ❧ Map N1 • Ulitsa Rozhdestvenka 12/1 • Metro: Kuznetskiy Most • Open noon–6am

9 Jao-Da
Featuring live alternative and ethnic music, Jao-Da serves European cuisine and a variety of teas. ❧ Map P3 • Lubyanskiy proezd 25 • (495) 623 2896 • Metro: Kitay Gorod • Open 24 hrs • Adm (for concerts only)

10 Loft
This trendy café's main draw is the sixth-floor view of the surrounding area from the summer terrace. ❧ Map N2 • Nautilus Shopping Mall, Lubyanskiy proezd 25 • (495) 933 7713 • Metro: Lubyanka • Open 9am–midnight

For details of the events hosted at Jao-Da visit http://jao-da.ru

Nostalgie Art Club

Price Categories

For a three-course meal for one with half a bottle of house wine (or equivalent meal).

R Under 800 Rub
RR 800–1,500 Rub
RRR 1,500–2,000 Rub
RRRR 2,000–2,500 Rub
RRRRR Over 2,500 Rub

☺ Restaurants

1 Annushka
A charming bar-restaurant on an old tram that makes circles of Chistye Prudy park every weekend. ✆ Map Q1 • Chistye Prudy tram line • Metro: Chistye Prudy • RR

2 Nostalgie Art Club
This Parisian-style restaurant offers high-class French cuisine and over 600 wines. ✆ Map Q2 • Chistoprudny Bulvar 12a • (495) 916 9478 • Metro: Chistye Prudy • RRRR

3 GlavPivTorg
GlavPivTorg serves a wide range of Russian dishes and vodkas in atmospheric surroundings. ✆ Map N1 • Ulitsa Bolshaya Lubyanka 5 • (495) 928 2591 • Metro: Kuznetskiy Most • RRRR

4 Expedition
Reindeer and polar penguin feature on the Siberian menu at the arctic-themed Expedition. ✆ Map Q3 • Pevcheskiy pereulok 6 • (495) 775 6075 • Metro: Kitay Gorod • RRRRR

5 Savoy
The sumptuous Savoy caters to an elite clientele, as it has done since 1913 (see p58). ✆ Map N2 • Ulitsa Rozhdestvenka 3 • (495) 929 8600 • Metro: Kuznetskiy Most • RRRRR

6 Dissident
This intimate restaurant specializes in European cuisine, with an excellent choice of wines and French cheeses. ✆ Map N2 • Nautilus Shopping Mall, Lubyanskiy proezd 25 • (495) 230 5848 • Metro: Lubyanka • RRRR

7 Noev Kovcheg
The Armenian dishes at "Noah's Ark" are best enjoyed with one of their Armenian brandies (see p59). ✆ Map Q3 • Malyy Ivanovskiy pereulok 9 • (495) 917 0717 • Metro: Kitay Gorod • RRRRR

8 Uzbekistan
Lavish oriental decor, belly dancers and a mix of Uzbek, Arabic and Chinese cuisine combine for an enjoyable evening (see p59). ✆ Map N1 • Ulitsa Neglinnaya 29 • (495) 623 0585 • Metro: Trubnaya • RRRRR

9 Boyarsky
Boyarsky has a magnificent church-like interior and specializes in traditional Russian dishes, such as stuffed quail. ✆ Map N2 • Metropol, Teatralnyy proezd 1/4 • (495) 270 1063 • Metro: Teatralnaya • RRRRR

10 Maharaja
At Maharaja, delicious Indian food is served in an understated yet elegant setting. ✆ Map Q2 • Ulitsa Pokrovka 2/1 • (495) 621 9844 • Metro: Kitay Gorod • RRR

Don't miss Nostalgie Art Club's 700-Rub (16-euro) business lunch served on weekdays from noon to 5pm.

Left **Melnikov House** Right **Tolstoy Literary Museum**

Arbatskaya

RADIATING WEST FROM THE CENTRE, *Ulitsas Arbat and Prechistenka* are two of Moscow's oldest streets. Both are lined with fine 19th-century mansions, built after the great fire that consumed most of the city's wooden architecture during Napoleon's invasion in 1812. The district became fashionable at this time, and wealthy aristocrats moved in along with a bohemian circle of artists, poets, musicians and writers who frequented Ulitsa Arbat's cafés and bars. After the six-lane Novyy Arbat was created in the 1960s, Ulitsa Arbat lost its importance and was neglected until the 1980s, when pedestrianization brought a new lease of life. Today the district boasts major museums, galleries and churches as well as shops, restaurants, clubs and bars.

Bustling Ulitsa Arbat

🔟 Sights

1. Ulitsa Arbat
2. Glazunov Gallery
3. Pushkin Museum of Fine Arts
4. Cathedral of Christ the Saviour
5. Skryabin House Museum
6. Tsereteli Gallery
7. Tolstoy Literary Museum
8. Pushkin House Museum
9. Melnikov House
10. Ministry of Foreign Affairs

1 Ulitsa Arbat

Since its pedestrianization, Ulitsa Arbat has become a bustling tourist attraction, lively with portrait painters, buskers and souvenir stalls. Along its length are several museum houses, a tiled Peace Wall designed by 7,000 children in 1990, statues of the poet Alexander Pushkin and his wife, and a bronze effigy of Bulat Okudzhava (1924–97) – a legendary underground poet and folk singer who immortalized the street with his song *My Arbat*. ◈ *Map K4 • Metro: Arbatskaya*

2 Glazunov Gallery

Occupying two floors of a 19th-century mansion, this gallery holds 3,000 paintings by Ilya Glazunov (b. 1930), a prolific artist and Rector of the Russian Academy of Painting, Sculpture and Architecture. Evocative pieces include *Decline* (2001), which portrays a drunk accordion player illuminated by a blood-red sun, and *The Great Experiment* (1990), featuring past and present political leaders, who look on while Moscow burns. ◈ *Map L5 • Ulitsa Volkhonka 13 • (495) 291 6949 • Metro: Kropotkinskaya • Open 11am–7pm Tue–Sun • Adm • www.glazunov.ru*

3 Pushkin Museum of Fine Arts

Home to the country's best collection of European art, the Pushkin Museum of Fine Arts complex has an exhibition of Ancient Egyptian Art and several halls of plaster cast copies of classical and Renaissance sculptures *(see pp16–17)*. The gallery's remarkable collection of Impressionist, post-Impressionist and Modernist paintings, including a large number of works by Pablo Picasso and Henri Matisse, are displayed in the adjacent Gallery of European and American Art of the 19th–20th Century *(see pp16–17)*.

4 Cathedral of Christ the Saviour

Tsar Alexander I commissioned the construction of Russia's largest Orthodox cathedral to mark the defeat of Napoleon in 1812. It was designed by the Russian architect Konstantin Ton (1794–1881) and completed in 1860, but was demolished in 1931 to make way for the Palace of the Soviets. That plan was later abandoned and in 1960, the spot was filled by the world's largest outdoor swimming pool. A fundraising campaign to rebuild the original cathedral followed the fall of Communism in 1991, and the existing replica was finished by 2000. ◈ *Map L5 • Ulitsa Volkhonka 15 • Metro: Kropotkinskaya • Open 10am–5pm • www.xxc.ru*

Cathedral of Christ the Saviour

Although the Gallery of European and American Art is part of the Pushkin Museum of Fine Arts, there is a separate admission fee.

5 Skryabin House Museum

The small mansion where Symbolist composer Aleksandr Skryabin (1872–1915) lived for three years before his death was opened as a state museum in 1922. On display is the ingenious coloured-light projector that Skryabin created for use with his *Prometheus* symphony. The museum hosts regular concerts at which Bechstein's custom-made grand piano can be heard. ⊗ *Map J4 • Bolshoy Nikolopeskovskiy pereulok 11 • (495) 241 1901 • Metro: Smolenskaya • Open noon–6pm Wed, Fri; noon–4pm Thu, Sat, Sun • Adm*

Interior of the Skryabin House Museum

6 Tsereteli Gallery

Opened in 2001, this gallery occupies a vast 19th-century mansion and exhibits works by Moscow's most influential and controversial artist, Zurab Tsereteli (b. 1934). Perhaps most striking is *Good Defeats Evil* – a massive bronze apple inside which visitors can step to trace the history of human passions since the Fall of Man. ⊗ *Map K6 • Ulitsa Prechistenka 19 • (495) 637 7679 • Metro: Park Kultury • Open noon–8pm Tue–Sun • Adm*

Bulat Okudzhava (1924–97)

Poet, singer and novelist Bulat Okudzhava became a legend in his own lifetime through the illegal distribution of his songs during the Soviet era; he is famous for his lyrics in the classic Russian film *White Sun of the Desert* (1969). Though he was careful not to criticize the regime overtly, his music was never recognized by the authorities.

7 Tolstoy Literary Museum

Established by the Tolstoy Society in 1911, a year after the author's death, this museum occupies a classically styled mansion designed by Afanasy Grigoriev in 1817. Its elegant rooms are filled with original copies of Tolstoy's manuscripts, first editions, photographs and personal effects. The collection includes *The Complete Works of Tolstoy* in 90 volumes, only available in Russian. ⊗ *Map K5 • Ulitsa Prechistenka 11 • (495) 202 2190 • Metro: Kropotkinskaya • 11am–6pm Tue–Sun • Adm • www.tolstoymuseum.ru*

8 Pushkin House Museum

Pushkin lived in this appealing blue mansion briefly after his marriage to Natalya Goncharova in 1831. It played host both to his stag night and their wedding reception. The

Caucasian Subject in the Tsereteli Gallery

A 20-minute film with rare footage of Tolstoy and his family at their summer estate is shown at the Tolstoy Literary Museum.

Exterior of the Pushkin House Museum

time the couple spent here was probably Pushkin's happiest; their later move to St Petersburg ultimately led to his fatal duel with her alleged lover. The museum was opened in 1986 and exhibits portraits, manuscripts and items of furniture belonging to the couple. ✪ *Map J4 • Ulitsa Arbat 53 • (495) 241 4212 • Metro: Smolenskaya • Open 10am–6pm Wed–Sun • Adm*

Melnikov House

9 Considered one of the 20th century's most original buildings, this intriguing house was built by Soviet architect Konstantin Melnikov as his home and studio between 1927 and 1929. It is not currently open to the public, although there are plans to convert it into a museum. ✪ *Map J4 • Krivoarbatskiy pereulok 10 • Metro: Smolenskaya • www.melnikovhouse.com*

Ministry of Foreign Affairs

10 One of Moscow's formidable Seven Sisters *(see pp46–7)*, the 172-m- (564-ft-) high Ministry of Foreign Affairs is a typical example of Stalinist design, and towers ominously over most of the surrounding buildings. Constructed between 1948 and 1953, it was initially flat roofed, but at Stalin's suggestion a metal spire was hastily added to bring its profile in line with those of its Sisters. ✪ *Map J5 • Smolenskaya-Sennaya Ploshchad 32–34 • Metro: Smolenskaya*

A Day Exploring Arbatskaya

Morning

🕐 Arriving at Kropotkinskaya, *(see p24)* stop to admire the station's spacious interior. Exit the station and head south towards the nearby **Cathedral of Christ the Saviour** *(see p75)*. Interior lifts whisk visitors up to the rooftop where glass galleries afford splendid views of the city. Next, stop at the small restaurant beside Kropotkinskaya station for coffee before visiting the **Pushkin Museum of Fine Arts** *(see p75)* across the road to the right. If it's a weekend or a holiday, be prepared for a long queue. If time is short, go across the street to visit the far smaller **Glazunov Gallery** *(see p75)* instead. After visiting the galleries, have lunch and a cocktail at the **Wall Street Bar** *(see p78)* before taking the metro to Smolenskaya.

Afternoon

At Smolenskaya note the station's theme of Russian military triumphs before exiting beneath the imposing **Ministry of Foreign Affairs**. Behind it stands a pair of Soviet-era hotels covered with state-of-the-art neon lighting. Begin walking along **Ulitsa Arbat**, pausing at the **Pushkin House Museum**. A right turn will take you to **Melnikov House**, a fascinating piece of avant-garde architecture. Return to Ulitsa Arbat to have your portrait painted or shop for souvenirs. Dine at the historic **Praga** restaurant *(see p79)* next to Arbatskaya Ploshchad, or head for **Elki-Palki** *(see p78)* on Novyy Arbat for traditional Russian fare.

Around Town – Arbatskaya

Left **Mu-Mu café** Centre **Sign outside Uncle Sam's Café** Right **Hard Rock Café**

🔟 Bars and Cafés

1 Mu-Mu
A popular self-service café, Mu-Mu serves fresh Russian salads and snacks in pleasant surroundings. ⊗ *Map K4 • Ulitsa Arbat 45/23 • (495) 241 1364 • Metro: Smolenskaya • Open 10am–11pm*

2 Yaposha
Part of a chain of popular Japanese eateries, Yaposha offers a range of sushi as well as good-value weekday lunches. ⊗ *Map K4 • Ulitsa Arbat 31 • (499) 241 0886 • Metro: Smolenskaya • Open 11am–11pm*

3 Sports Bar
A modern bar with two large screens and sporting memorabilia. ⊗ *Map K3 • Ulitsa Novyy Arbat 10 • (495) 690 4311 • Metro: Arbatskaya • Open 11am–5am*

4 Yolki-Palki
This traditional-style Russian pub features stuffed chickens, plastic vines and salad bar wagons. ⊗ *Map K3 • Ulitsa Novyy Arbat 11 • (495) 291 6888 • Metro: Arbatskaya • Open 11am–11pm*

5 Uncle Sam's Café
An American-themed café with plenty of cocktails and Marilyn Monroe posters on the walls. ⊗ *Map K4 • Ulitsa Arbat 23 • (495) 697 5695 • Metro: Arbatskaya • Open noon–5:30am*

6 Hard Rock Café
Occupying an old mansion, the Hard Rock Café features the usual musical memorabilia.

⊗ *Map J4 • Ulitsa Arbat 44 • (495) 241 4342 • Metro: Smolenskaya • Open 9am–midnight Mon–Thu, 9–4am Fri–Sun*

7 Gogol Mogol
Gogol Mogol is a Parisian-style café with exquisite desserts and snacks. ⊗ *Map K5 • Gagarinskiy pereulok 6 • (495) 695 1131 • Metro: Kropotkinskaya • Open 10am–11pm*

8 Tinkoff
A modern pub-restaurant, Tinkoff brews its own range of beers on site. ⊗ *Map D4 • Protochnyy pereulok 11 • (495) 777 3300 • Metro: Kuznetskiy Most • Open noon–2am*

9 Wall Street Bar
An upmarket bar serving faultless cocktails. Late-night DJs are an added attraction. ⊗ *Map L4 • Ulitsa Volkhonka 9/1 • (495) 916 5731 • Metro: Kropotkinskaya • Open 11–2am*

10 Plotnikov Pub
Plotnikov offers whiskies and Irish and German beers. ⊗ *Map J4 • Plotnikov pereulok 22/16 • (495) 241 8799 • Metro: Smolenskaya • Open 11am–11pm*

Yolki-Palki is part of a hugely successful chain owned by Moscow's top restaurateur, Arkady Novikov.

Price Categories

For a three-course meal for one with half a bottle of house wine (or equivalent meal).

R	Under 800 Rub
RR	800–1,500 Rub
RRR	1,500–2,000 Rub
RRRR	2,000–2,500 Rub
RRRRR	Over 2,500 Rub

Exterior of the chic Kupol

Restaurants

1 Kupol
Ultra-stylish, glass-roofed Kupol serves intriguing dishes, such as asparagus soup with truffle ice cream and sweet glazed tuna steak. ⊗ *Map C3*
• *Novyy Arbat 36* • *(495) 690 7373*
• *Metro: Arbatskaya* • *RRRRR*

2 Praga
This historic restaurant is acclaimed for its classy cuisine and opulent decor. ⊗ *Map K3*
• *Ulitsa Arbat 2/1* • *(495) 690 6171*
• *Metro: Arbatskaya* • *RRRRR*

3 Cantinetta Antinori
An exclusive restaurant featuring some of the best wines in town. ⊗ *Map J5*
• *Denezhnyy pereulok 20* • *(499) 241 3325* • *Metro: Smolenskaya* • *RRRRR*

4 Genatsvale na Arbat
This authentic Georgian restaurant features great food and live Georgian folk music. ⊗ *Map K3* • *Novyy Arbat 11/2* • *(495) 203 9453* • *Metro: Arbatskaya* • *RRRRR*

5 Vstochny Kvartal
Decorated with wood panelling and oriental furnishings, this atmospheric Uzbek restaurant serves excellent food. ⊗ *Map J4* • *Ulitsa Arbat 45/24* • *(499) 241 3803* • *Metro: Smolenskaya* • *RRRRR*

6 Kish-Mish
Done up in the style of a traditional Uzbek house, Kish-Mish offers classic Uzbek dishes, such as marinated lamb and freshly baked sesame bread.
⊗ *Map K4* • *Novyy Arbat 28/2* • *(495) 291 2010* • *Metro: Smolenskaya* • *RRR*

7 Grand Imperial
This restaurant boasts flawless international cuisine within a magnificent interior. ⊗ *Map K5*
• *Gagarinskiy pereulok 9/5* • *(495) 291 6063* • *Metro: Kropotkinskaya* • *RRRRR*

8 San Marco
The international menu here includes rabbit with pumpkin and duck with cranberry sauce. ⊗ *Map K4* • *Ulitsa Arbat 25* • *(495) 291 7089*
• *Metro: Arbatskaya* • *RRRRR*

9 5-Spice
One of the best Chinese restaurants in town, 5-Spice serves Cantonese dishes. ⊗ *Map K4* • *Sivtev Vrazhek pereulok 3/18* • *(495) 203 1283* • *Metro: Kropotkinskaya* • *R*

10 Tiflis
Expect impeccable service and superb cuisine at this classy Georgian restaurant *(see p58)*. ⊗ *Map K6* • *Ulitsa Ostozhenka 32* • *(499) 766 9728* • *Metro: Kropotkinskaya* • *RRRR*

Tiflis has a delightful outdoor dining area shaded by vines, which is perfect in summer.

Left **Iconostasis in the Upper Monastery of St Peter** Right **Chekhov House Museum**

Tverskaya

THIS VIBRANT DISTRICT *takes its name from Ulitsa Tverskaya, the historic street used by royal processions travelling from the Kremlin to the once-powerful city of Tver. It has long been both a thriving commercial centre and fashionable residential district. Although it was one of the few quarters to escape significant damage during the Fire of Moscow in 1812, its original wooden architecture was replaced in the late 19th century by elegant apartment blocks and mansions, which now stand side-by-side with anonymous concrete housing and office blocks erected during the Soviet era.*

🔟 Sights

1. Bolshoy Theatre
2. Museum of Modern Art
3. Museum of Modern History
4. Moscow Art Theatre
5. Sanduny Bath House
6. Upper Monastery of St Peter
7. Gulag Museum
8. Bulgakov Museum
9. Chekhov House Museum
10. Gorky House Museum

Sumptuous interior of the Bolshoy Theatre

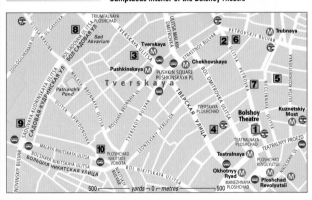

Preceding pages **Ulitsa Arbat in winter**

Bolshoy Theatre

The Bolshoy, one of the city's most famous landmarks, is undergoing major repairs to restore it to its full glory, and is expected to be fully open by 2011. In the meantime, its world-class opera and ballet companies continue to thrill audiences in the adjacent New Bolshoy Theatre, with their performances of classics such as *Don Quixote* and *Eugene Onegin*, as well as new productions *(see pp18–19)*.

Museum of Modern Art

Most of this substantial collection of Russian modern art belongs to prolific artist and director of the Russian Academy of Arts, Zurab Tsereteli, who opened the museum with the backing of Yuri Luzhkov, the mayor of Moscow. Housed in an 18th-century building designed by Russian architect Matvey Kazakov, the gallery exhibits works by Pablo Picasso and Joan Miro, as well as Russian modernists including Kazimir Malevich and Wassily Kandinsky. ◈ *Map M1 • Ulitsa Petrovka 25 • (495) 694 2890 • Metro: Chekhovskaya • Open noon–8pm • Adm (free Mon–Wed) • www.mmoma.ru*

Museum of Modern History

Charting the country's history from the early 19th century to the present, the museum's collection fills the extravagant halls of a mansion once known as the English Club, a high-class meeting place for foreigners in pre-Revolution Moscow. Among the exhibits is military equipment dating back to the disastrous Russo-Japanese War of 1904–5, and weapons used in street fights during the 1905 Russian Revolution. The exhibition culminates with a proud display of the country's recent industrial successes.
◈ *Map L1 • Ulitsa Tverskaya 21 • (495) 699 6724 • Metro: Tverskaya • Open 10am–6pm Tue, Wed, Fri; 11am–7pm Thu, Sat • Adm • www.sovr.ru*

Moscow Art Theatre

Founded in 1898 by method acting pioneer Konstantin Stanislavski (1863–1938) and playwright Vladimir Nemirovich-Danchenko (1858–1943), the Moscow Art Theatre earned its reputation through successful performances of Maxim Gorky's early plays and Anton Chekhov's play *The Seagull*. Today the theatre puts on a broad repertoire of Russian and international plays. The upstairs theatre museum displays costumes and props used in 20th-century productions.
◈ *Map M2 • Kamergerskiy pereulok 3 • (495) 629 8760 • Metro: Teatralnaya, Okhotnyy Ryad • Open 11am–7pm (ticket office) • Adm • http://art.theatre.ru*

Imposing façade of the Moscow Art Theatre

The waiting area inside the luxurious Sanduny Bath House

of Metropolitan Peter, built in 1517 by the Italian architect Alvesio Lamberti. The church's original frescoes have recently been restored, as have those of the 17th-century Refectory Church. ◎ *Map M1*
• *Corner of Ulitsa Petrovka and Petrovskiy Bulvar*
• *Metro: Chekhovskaya*
• *Open 8am–8pm*

Sanduny Bath House

Built in 1896, Moscow's most famous bath house has a well-restored interior featuring Italian marble columns, chandeliers, stained glass windows and classical sculptures. It still functions as a bath recreation complex. ◎ *Map N1* • *Ulitsa Neglinnaya 14/3–7* • *(495) 625 4631* • *Metro: Trubnaya* • *Open 8am–10pm* • *Adm* • *www.sanduny.ru*

Upper Monastery of St Peter

Founded in the late 14th century, this monastery once formed part of Moscow's outer defences. Sheltering behind its high red walls are gardens and several pretty churches, the oldest of which is the single-domed Church

Gulag Museum

The museum's tiny exhibition is a memorial to the estimated 20 million citizens who were jailed or executed for political offences during the Soviet era. The ground floor has a mock-up of a camp barracks, while upstairs are artworks by gulag survivors along with photographs, newspaper articles and a map indicating the location of over 500 of Russia's gulags. ◎ *Map M1* • *Ulitsa Petrovka 16* • *(495) 621 7346* • *Metro: Okhotnyy Ryad* • *Open 11am–4pm Tue–Sat* • *Adm* • *www. museum-gulag.narod.ru*

Bulgakov Museum

The former flat of Russia's celebrated author Mikhail Bulgakov (1891–1940) has long been a pilgrimage site for his fans and was recently turned into a museum. Bulgakov lived here from 1921 to 1924, and this is where he wrote the draft of his epic novel *The Master and Margarita*, in which he incorporated the number 50 (his own apartment number) as the address of the devil's residence. The museum contains personal effects, photographs and copies of his manuscripts. ◎ *Map K1* • *Ulitsa Bolshaya Sadovaya 10, Apt 50* • *(495) 699 5366* • *Metro: Mayakovskaya* • *Open 1–11pm Sun–Thu, 1pm–1am Fri–Sat* • *Adm*

Ancient Tver

The medieval citadel of Tver lay 170 km (106 miles) northwest of Moscow and came close to eclipsing the capital in the 14th century, but ultimately yielded to its rival after suffering successive defeats. In 1941 it was burned to the ground by Nazi forces, and though it has since been rebuilt, no trace of its grand history remains.

The Bulgakov Museum organizes regular literary events as well as walking tours of the area.

9 Chekhov House Museum

Though Anton Chekhov (1860–1904) lived in this modest house for only four years between 1886 and 1890, he is thought to have written some of his best works here. Despite early success as a writer, he continued practising as a doctor and his consultation rooms have been preserved within the museum. Other exhibits include some first editions of his books and an array of colourful posters announcing performances of his plays at the Moscow Art Theatre. ◈ Map J2 • Ulitsa Sadovaya-Kudrinskaya 6 • (495) 691 6154 • Metro: Barrikadnaya • Open 11am–6pm Tue, Thu, Sat–Sun; 2–9pm Wed, Fri

10 Gorky House Museum

A magnificent example of Art Nouveau architecture, Gorky House is a visual feast of flowing asymmetrical motifs. It was given to writer and Soviet propagandist Maxim Gorky (1868–1936) by Stalin upon the writer's return to the Soviet Union in 1931. Gorky's library, letters, manuscripts and some personal belongings are all on display. ◈ Map K2 • Ulitsa Malaya Nikitskaya 6/2 • (495) 690 0535 • Metro: Tverskaya • Open 11am–6pm Wed–Sun

The Art Nouveau Gorky House Museum

A Day Out in Historic Tverskaya

Morning

🕐 Start at Okhotnyy Ryad metro station and head away from the Kremlin along **Ulitsa Tverskaya**, passing the grand **Le Royal Meridian National** (see p116), on your left, where Lenin stayed after the Russian Revolution. To the right is the **State Duma** building. A little further on is Kamergersky pereulok, where a statue of Chekhov stands outside the **Moscow Art Theatre** (see p83). Visit the theatre museum upstairs. Return to Ulitsa Tverskaya and continue towards the **Maki Café** on Glinitchevskiy pereulok for a cup of herbal tea before heading for the historic **Yeliseyevskiy Food Hall** (see p86) on Ulitsa Tverskaya to admire its architecture. Further up the street is the **Museum of Modern History** (see p83) which has a café where you can stop for lunch.

Afternoon

Head east along Strastnoy Bulvar past Pushkinskaya Ploshchad and the Soviet-era Pushkinskiy cinema to reach the **Upper Monastery of St Peter**. The **Museum of Modern Art** (see p83) stands opposite. From there, stroll down **Ulitsa Petrovka** past trendy boutiques and pre-Revolution mansions, looking out for the **Petrovskiy Pasazh**, on the left, with its chic boutiques and a café. You can either return to Ulitsa Petrovka and visit the **Gulag Museum** and the **Bolshoy Theatre** (see p83), or continue through Petrovskiy Pasazh and turn left onto Ulitsa Neglinnaya. Relax at the **Sanduny Bath House**, a short walk away.

Left **A shop on Ulitsa Kuznetskiy Most** Centre **Manezh Mall** Right **Yeliseyevskiy Food Hall**

🔟 Places to Shop

1 Ulitsa Tverskaya
One of the city's main shopping streets, Ulitsa Tverskaya is home to malls, museums, shops and restaurants *(see p53)*. ⊗ Map L1 • Metro: Tverskaya, Mayakovskaya

2 Ulitsa Petrovka
Many of Ulitsa Petrovka's smart 19th-century buildings are now occupied by chic boutiques, including Fred Perry and Sergio Rossi *(see p52)*. ⊗ Map M1 • Metro: Teatralnaya

3 Galereya Aktyor
This mall contains a mixture of designer clothing and jewellery stores that are upmarket but not exclusive. ⊗ Map L1 • Ulitsa Tverskaya 16 • Metro: Tverskaya • Open 10am–8pm

4 Petrovskiy Pasazh
This gleaming mall features a handful of exclusive boutiques. ⊗ Map M1 • Ulitsa Petrovka • Metro: Tverskaya • Open 11am–8pm

5 Transylvania
With a wide range of CDs and DVDs, this store is one of the best in town for vintage and specialist music. ⊗ Map L1 • Ulitsa Tverskaya 6/1, Bldg 5 • (495) 629 8786 • Metro: Mayakovskaya • Open 11am–9pm

6 Ulitsa Kuznetskiy Most
This quiet street is lined with charming 19th-century buildings housing exclusive boutiques, such as Versace, Cartier and Ferre. ⊗ Map N2 • Ulitsa Kuznetskiy Most • Metro: Kuznetskiy Most

7 TsUM
Opened in 1857, this major department store has seven floors of designer goods *(see p53)*. ⊗ Map N2 • Ulitsa Petrovka 2 • Metro: Teatralnaya • Open 10am–10pm • www.tsum.ru

8 Manezh Mall
The Manezh is filled with mainstream outlets and has a food court on its lower floor *(see p52)*. ⊗ Map M3 • Manezhnaya Ploshchad 1 • Metro: Okhotnyy Ryad • 10am–11pm

9 Yeliseyevskiy Food Hall
This historic food market, dating back to the 1900s, has a breathtaking interior. ⊗ Map L1 • Ulitsa Tverskaya 14 • Metro: Tverskaya • Open 10am–8pm

10 Museum of Modern History Souvenir Shop
The museum's shop sells original Soviet memorabilia, including military accessories *(see p83)*. ⊗ Map L1 • Ulitsa Tverskaya 21 • Metro: Tverskaya • Open 11am–6pm Tue–Sat

Price Categories
For a three-course meal for one with half a bottle of house wine (or equivalent meal).

R	Under 800 Rub
RR	800–1,500 Rub
RRR	1,500–2,000 Rub
RRRR	2,000–2,500 Rub
RRRRR	Over 2,500 Rub

Café des Artistes

🔟 Cafés and Restaurants

1 Café Pushkin
Classic French cuisine is served at this elegant café *(see p58)*. ◈ *Map L1 • Tverskoy Bulvar 26a • (495) 629 5590 • Metro: Pushkinskaya • RRRRR*

2 Pavilion
Pavilion serves exquisitely presented dishes in a fine building overlooking Patriarch's Pond. ◈ *Map K1 • Bolshoy Patriarshiy pereulok • (495) 697 5110 • Metro: Mayakovskaya • RRRR*

3 Zhan-Zhak Café
This delightful Parisian-style café offers great French cuisine and a wine list. ◈ *Map L3 • Nikitskiy Bulvar 12 • (495) 690 3886 • Metro: Arbatskaya • RRR*

4 Nedalny Vostok
Top restauranteur Arkady Novikov's Asian fusion project marries Russian *pelmeni* (filled dumplings) with Japanese scallops. ◈ *Map L2 • Ulitsa Tverskoy Bulvar 15/2 • (495) 694 0641 • Metro: Pushkinskaya • RRRRR*

5 Café des Artistes
This elegant café-restaurant has a fine menu and doubles as an art gallery. ◈ *Map M2 • Kamergskiy pereulok 5/6 • (495) 692 4042 • Metro: Okhotnyy Ryd • RRRRR*

6 Donna Klara
A popular French-style café, Donna Klara serves great coffee and a delicious selection of pastries, sweets and cakes. ◈ *Map K1 • Ulitsa Malaya Bronnaya 21/13 • (495) 290 3848 • Metro: Pushkinskaya • RRR*

7 Maki Café
This simple café has quickly gained popularity, dishing up inexpensive food amid unpretentious surroundings. ◈ *Map L1 • Glinishchevskiy pereulok 3 • (495) 692 9731 • Metro: Pushkinskaya • RR*

8 Café Margarita
This French-style café-bar has hearty soups and salads. ◈ *Map K1 • Ulitsa Malaya Bronnaya 28 • (495) 699 6534 • Metro: Pushkinskaya • RRR*

9 Bacchus Bar
A traditional-style pub, Bacchus offers English, German, Czech and Russian beers. ◈ *Map K1 • Ulitsa Malaya Bronnaya 20a • (495) 650 6463 • Metro: Pushkinskaya • RR*

10 Sinbad
This Lebanese café has hookah pipes and inexpensive food. ◈ *Map K2 • Nikitskiy Bulvar 14 • (495) 691 7115 • Metro: Arbatskaya • RR*

The first scene of Bulgakov's novel The Master and Margarita *(see p42)* is set by the pond opposite Café Margarita, hence its name.

Left **Exterior, New Tretyakov Gallery** Right **Lenin's Funeral Train Museum**

Zamoskvoreche

ZAMOSKVORECHE WAS SETTLED *in the 15th century by merchants and artisans, and many of its streets still bear the names of their trades. Prone to flooding, much of the land was given over to industry and farming. During the 19th century a canal was dug to prevent the floods and several large estates were established. These were built by wealthy merchants, such as the Tretyakov brothers and Aleksey Bakhrushin, who contributed enormously to the flourishing cultural scene for which Zamoskvoreche remains known today.*

Church of St Gregory of Neocaesarea

Visitors admiring the collection at the Tretyakov Gallery

🔟 Sights

1. Tretyakov Gallery
2. New Tretyakov Gallery
3. Church of the Resurrection in Kadashi
4. Ostrovskiy House Museum
5. Bakhrushin Theatre Museum
6. Gorky Park
7. Lenin's Funeral Train Museum
8. Socialist Sculpture Park
9. Historic Mosque
10. Church of St Gregory of Neocaesarea

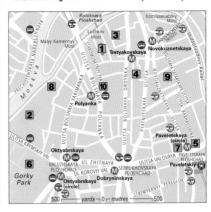

Tretyakov Gallery

Spanning Russian art history from the earliest medieval icons to Impressionist works of the late 19th century, the Tretyakov Gallery boasts a phenomenal collection *(see pp20–23)*.

New Tretyakov Gallery

This 20th-century collection brings together officially accepted Socialist Realism artworks and pieces produced "underground" in the same period, by artists who were sidelined as a result of their refusal to compromise. The gallery occupies several floors of the concrete block it shares with the Central House of Artists *(see p92)*. Rumour has it that the government plans to replace the building with an ultra-modern complex in the shape of a peeled orange, designed by controversial UK architect Lord Foster.
◈ *Map E5 • Ulitsa Krymskiy val • (499) 230 7788 • Metro: Park Kultury • Open 10am–7:30pm Tue–Sun • Adm*
• *www.tretyakovgallery.ru*

Church of the Resurrection in Kadashi

Funded by public subscription in the 17th century, this glorious Moscow Baroque church has recently undergone major restoration, following the eviction of the furniture factory that had occupied it since 1964. The church earlier fell victim to Napoleon's troops, who stabled their horses here before setting fire to the building upon their retreat in 1812. Work is currently underway on restoration of the interior but, paradoxically, property developers have

Church of the Resurrection in Kadashi

been granted permission to build a luxury residential complex that will surround the church on three sides. ◈ *Map N5 • 2-oy Kadashevskiy pereulok 7 • Metro: Novokuznetskaya • Open 6–8pm*

Ostrovskiy House Museum

Surrounded by pleasant gardens, this charming house is where Russian Realist playwright Aleksandr Ostrovskiy (1823–86) was born and raised. Ostrovskiy gained fame for his early satirical comedies and later penned over 47 plays, which were performed at Moscow's Maly Theatre. His play *The Snow Maiden* has been in the Bolshoy Opera Company's repertoire since 2002. A rare example of Moscow's 19th-century wooden architecture, the house is filled with manuscripts, photographs and the family's furniture.
◈ *Map N6 • Ulitsa Malaya Ordynka 9 • (495) 953 8684 • Metro: Tretyakovskaya • Open noon–7pm Wed–Sun • Adm*

Ostrovskiy House Museum

Lovers' Bridge

On the footbridge linking Lavrushinskiy pereulok with Balchug Island is a delightful sight: a series of metal trees festooned with padlocks. Newlyweds add their own locks, marked with their wedding date, to secure their love forever. The practice is said to have originated at the Great Wall of China, where couples hang padlocks on special chains.

Bakhrushin Theatre Museum

This museum was built in 1896 to house the theatrical memorabilia of the wealthy philanthropist Aleksey Bakhrushin (1865–1929). Exhibits include historic playbills, costumes and set designs used in 19th- and 20th-century theatre performances.
⊗ Map G5 • Ulitsa Bakhrushina 31/12 • (495) 953 4470 • Metro: Paveletskaya • Open noon–7pm Wed–Mon • Adm

A set design on display at the Bakhrushin Theatre Museum

Gorky Park

Russia's first theme park, set along the banks of the Moskva river, was opened in 1928. Entered via a monumental arch adorned with hammer and sickle emblems, the park is a lovely expanse of gardens packed with family-friendly activities.
⊗ Map E6 • Ulitsa Krymsky val 9 • Metro: Park Kultury • Open 11am–8pm

Lenin's Funeral Train Museum

The funeral train that pulled Lenin's body from his country house to Moscow in January 1924 is housed in a grand museum hall behind Paveletskiy railway station. The solemn black train has a bold red star on its boiler and pulls a single windowless carriage. ⊗ Map G6 • Paveletskiy railway station • Metro: Paveletskaya • Open 10am–6pm Tue–Sun

Socialist Sculpture Park

Used as a dumping ground for Communist statues after the collapse of the Soviet Union in 1991, the Sculpture Park was officially opened in 1992. With the abandoned statues forming the core, the collection has grown to more than 700, including a

Boating on the lake, Gorky Park

The Bakhrushin Theatre Museum has a room dedicated to the legendary Russian opera singer Fyodor Shalyapin (1873–1938).

Statue of Trotsky, Socialist Sculpture Park

statue of Leon Trotsky. The park's most infamous resident is a statue of Stalin, whose nose has been broken by vandals. ✆ *Map M6 • Ulitsa Krymskiy val 10 • Metro: Park Kultury • Open 9am–8pm • Adm*

9 Historic Mosque

Permission to construct Moscow's oldest mosque was granted in 1823, on condition that no minarets were added. In 1936, the Soviet regime executed the mosque's *imam* (prayer leader) and went on to turn the building into a printing factory. The mosque re-opened in 1993 and today serves some of Moscow's 1-million-strong Muslim community. ✆ *Map P5 • Ulitsa Tatarskaya 28 • Metro: Novokuznetskaya • Open 7am–10pm*

10 Church of St Gregory of Neocaesarea

Tsar Alexis ordered the construction of this ornate church in 1668 upon the site of a 15th-century chapel. A famous "peacock eye" frieze encircles the roof, while inside is a gilt iconostasis and a copy of the miraculous icon of Our Lady of Kykkos. Closed during Communism, the church re-opened in 1996. ✆ *Map M6 • Ulitsa Bolshaya Polyanka • Metro: Polyanka • Open 8am–7:30pm*

An Art-Lover's Tour of Zamoskvoreche

Morning

🕐 Start at Park Kultury metro station and cross the Moskva river over Krymskiy Bridge. From here Tsereteli's **Peter the Great statue** is visible to your left, as is the **Cathedral of Christ the Saviour** (*see p75*). Cross the river and descend the steps towards the concrete building that houses the **Central House of Artists** and the **New Tretyakov Gallery** (*see p89*). Have lunch at the Central House of Artists' smart café before exploring the **Socialist Sculpture Park**. If you prefer being outside, bypass the galleries and turn right under the underpass (lined with art stalls) towards the arched entrance to **Gorky Park**, which has plenty of places to eat and relax. In summer, boats operate city tours from the Gorky Park river station.

Afternoon

From Gorky Park continue along Krymskiy val to Oktyabrskaya metro station. Take the metro to Tretyakovskaya and spend an afternoon at the nearby **Tretyakov Gallery**. Its café makes a good snack stop. Continue up Lavrushinskiy pereulok towards the river, pausing to admire the **Church of the Resurrection in Kadashi** (*see p89*), before crossing the **Lovers' Bridge**. Follow the river west towards the Peter the Great statue. The large building across the Maly Kamenny bridge was once home to the famous Red October Chocolate Factory and is now partially used by the **ArtStrelka Gallery** (*see p92*) to host contemporary art shows.

 From the Socialist Sculpture Park you can see Zurab Tsereteli's striking statue of Peter the Great, set on an island in the river.

Left **Paintings for sale at the Art Market** Right **Artworks at the Central House of Artists**

1 Central House of Artists

An arts centre filled with private galleries *(see p38)*. 🔍 *Map E5 • Ulitsa Krymskiy val 10 • (499) 238 9843 • Metro: Park Kultury • Open 11am–8pm Tue–Sun • Adm • www.cha.ru*

2 Marat Guelman Gallery

Cutting-edge shows by new Russian artists *(see p39)*. 🔍 *Map E5 • Ulitsa Malaya Polyanka 7/7, Bldg 5 • (495) 238 8492 • Metro: Polyanka • Open noon–8pm Tue–Sun • www.guelman.ru*

3 Red Art and Filimonoff Gallery

Abstract sculptures and paintings by Russian artists. 🔍 *Map E5 • Central House of Artists, Room NG13 • (495) 238 63 22 • Metro: Park Kultury • Open 11am–7pm Tue–Sun*

4 ArtStrelka Gallery

Home to many contemporary galleries hosting regular exhibitions. 🔍 *Map L5 • Berenevskaya nab. 14/5 • Metro: Kropotkinskaya • Open 4–8pm • www.artstrelka.ru*

5 TV Gallery

An innovative gallery putting on video and TV art shows. 🔍 *Map M6 • Ulitsa Bolshaya Yakimanka 6 • (495) 238 0269 • Metro: Polyanka • Open noon–7pm Tue–Sat • www.tvgallery.ru*

6 Krokin Gallery

This stylish gallery presents graphic art, multimedia and photography exhibitions. 🔍 *Map M6 • Ulitsa Bolshaya Polyanka 15 • Metro: Polyanka • Open 11am–7pm • www.krokingallery.com*

7 Lumiere Photo Gallery

This gallery houses an extensive collection of old and new images by Russian photographers. 🔍 *Map E5 • Central House of Artists, Room A51 • (495) 238 7753 • Metro: Park Kultury • Open 11am–7pm Tue–Sun • www.lumiere.ru*

8 Alla Bulyanskaya Gallery

Abstract bronze sculptures, expressionist canvases and surreal works by contemporary Russian artists. 🔍 *Map E5 • Central House of Artists, Room NG7 • (499) 238 2589 • Metro: Park Kultury • Open noon–7pm Tue–Sun • www.allabulgallery.com*

9 Melarus Gallery

This gallery features landscapes, portraits and still lifes with Russian folk motifs. 🔍 *Map E5 • Central House of Artists, Room 42 • Metro: Park Kultury • Open 11am–8pm Tue–Sun*

10 Art Market

A long underpass crammed with stalls selling original artworks at great prices. 🔍 *Map E5 • Underpass between Gorky Park and New Tretyakov • Metro: Park Kultury • Open 10am–8pm Tue–Sun*

For information on other galleries in Moscow See pp38–9.

Price Categories

For a three-course meal for one with half a bottle of house wine (or equivalent meal).

R Under 800 Rub
RR 800–1,500 Rub
RRR 1,500–2,000 Rub
RRRR 2,000–2,500 Rub
RRRRR Over 2,500 Rub

Left **Interior, Suliko restaurant** Right **Correa's restaurant**

Cafés and Restaurants

Suliko
Suliko has a vast Georgian menu. Bread is baked on site and there is also a selection of delicious home-made wines. ◎ Map F6 • Ulitsa Bolshaya Polyanka 42 • (499) 238 2888 • Metro: Polyanka • RRR

Dorian Gray
One of the city's best Italian restaurants (see p59). ◎ Map M5 • Kadashevskaya nab. 6/1 • (495) 238 6401 • Metro: Tretyakovskaya • RRRR

Observatoire
This exclusive restaurant offers tremendous international cuisine. Reservations essential. ◎ Map M6 • Bolshaya Yakimanka 22/3 • (495) 643 3606 • Metro: Polyanka • RRRRR

Matreshka
With a thatched ceiling and rough wooden tables, this traditional Russian diner exudes rural simplicity. ◎ Map N6 • Klimentovskiy pereulok 10/2 • (495) 953 9400 • Metro: Tretyakovskaya • RRR

Correa's
Run by an American expatriate, Correa's serves Italian cuisine in an informal setting. ◎ Map F6 • Ulitsa Bolshaya Ordynka 40/2 • (495) 725 6035 • Metro: Polyanka • RR

William Bass
This English-style pub is favoured by expatriates, offering steak and chips, real ales, cider and football on a big screen. ◎ Map M6 • Ulitsa Malaya Yakimanka 9 • (495) 778 1874 • Metro: Polyanka • RRR

Oblomov
Serving old Russian favourites such as *pelmeni* (dumplings) and smoked fish, Oblomov allows a glimpse into aristocratic life in pre-Revolution Russia (see p59). ◎ Map F6 • 1st Monetchikovskiy pereulok 5 • (495) 953 6828 • Metro: Dobryninskaya • RRRRR

Kvartira 44
Full of fascinating characters, this atmospheric, bohemian bar offers a mixture of Russian and Italian dishes served in generous portions. ◎ Map M6 • Ulitsa Malaya Yakimanka 24/8 • (495) 238 8234 • Metro: Polyanka • RR

Shesh Besh
A Turkish restaurant with rural-style decor and a popular all-you-can-eat salad bar. ◎ Map N5 • Ulitsa Pyatnishkaya 24/1 • (495) 959 5862 • Metro: Tretyakovskaya • RR

Mi Piace
Part of a small chain of mid-range Italian restaurants, Mi Piace serves up delicious pizzas. Ask for a table in the courtyard. ◎ Map N6 • Ulitsa Bolshaya Ordynka 13/9 • (495) 951 5250 • Metro: Tretyakovskaya • RRR

Left **Novospasskiy Monastery** Right **Museum of the Great Patriotic War**

Greater Moscow

ENSCONCED BETWEEN THE FEATURELESS MASS *of Soviet housing estates cluttering the suburbs beyond Moscow's Garden Ring are a surprising number of green spaces and tourist attractions, perfect for brief escapes from the hectic city centre. Many of the parks were once home to the grand summer estates of Moscow's aristocratic elite; they conceal architectural gems, such as the palaces of Ostankino and Kuskovo, which have been preserved as museums. South of the city are several fortified monasteries and convents, some founded as early as the 13th century; these shelter pretty churches and cathedrals behind formidable walls, built to defend the city from invading Poles, Tatars and Mongols.*

The Grotto on the Kuskovo Estate

🔟 Sights

1. Kolomenskoe Estate
2. Kuskovo Estate
3. Novodevichiy Convent and Cemetery
4. Borodino Panorama Museum
5. All-Russian Exhibition Centre (VVTs)
6. Victory Monument and Museum of the Great Patriotic War
7. Lyublino Estate
8. Novospasskiy Monastery
9. Moscow State University
10. Tolstoy House Museum

1 Kolomenskoe Estate

The favourite summer retreat for a succession of tsars between the 16th and 18th centuries, Kolomenskoe still draws picnicking Muscovites on weekends and holidays. Among its many attractions is the *troika* ride around the grounds *(see pp28–9)*.

Mead brewery on the Kolomenskoe Estate

2 Kuskovo Estate

One of 1,200 villages owned by the Sheremetev family, this idyllic estate was developed into a summer residence in the 18th century. Several talented architects were chosen from among the family's 200,000 serfs to design the ensemble of buildings. Its centrepiece is the wooden Kuskovo Palace, with a lavish interior featuring materials from all over Europe. The 18th-century Grotto, with an ornate interior adorned with shells and porcelain, is the most striking of Kuskovo's pavilions. ⊗ *Map B2 • Ulitsa Yunost 2 • (495) 370 0150 • Metro: Ryazanskiy Prospekt • Nov–March: 10am–4pm Wed–Sun; Apr–Oct: 10am–6pm Wed–Sun • Adm*

3 Novodevichiy Convent and Cemetery

Founded in the 16th century both as a convent and a defensive fortress, today Novodevichiy also includes several pretty 17th-century churches and a museum. Outside its walls is the famous cemetery where prominent figures lie buried *(see pp26–7)*.

4 Borodino Panorama Museum

The main highlight of this cylindrical museum is a panoramic painting entitled *The Battle of Borodino*. Commissioned for the centenary of Russia's Patriotic War against France, the painting depicts Napoleon's cavalry attack in 1812 *(see p96)*. It lacked a permanent home until 1962, when this museum was opened. The exhibition also charts the progress and retreat of Napoleon's armies and includes original military uniforms, weapons and banners. ⊗ *Map A5 • Kutuzovskiy proezd 38 • (499) 148 1967 • Metro: Kutuzovskaya • Open 10am–6pm Sat–Thu • Adm*

The Novodevichiy Convent and Cemetery

The Triumphal Arch at the entrance to the All-Russian Exhibition Centre (VVTs)

5 All-Russian Exhibition Centre (VVTs)

First opened in 1939 to showcase the USSR's agricultural achievements, this centre soon became a focal point for exhibitions. Over 80 massive pavilions were constructed, each adorned with Soviet sculptures and dedicated to a particular field of technology. Today many of the pavilions have been turned into shops, and amusement parks provide an added attraction. ◈ *Map B1 • Mira Prospekt • Metro: VDNKh • Open 9am–7pm (grounds), 10am–6pm (pavilions)*

6 Victory Monument and Museum of the Great Patriotic War

Opened in 1995 to mark the 50th anniversary of the end of the Great Patriotic War (World War II), this vast memorial museum is watched over by a sculpture of Nike, set on top of a 141-m (463-ft) obelisk that dominates the centre of Victory Park. Within the museum grounds is an exhibition of military vehicles and equipment. ◈ *Map A2 • Kutuzovskiy Prospekt • (495) 449 8159 • Metro: Kutuzovskaya • Open 10am–7pm Tue–Sun • Adm*

7 Lyublino Estate

This idyllic estate was bought by Nikolai Durasov in 1800 and developed into a grand complex of buildings. The centrepiece of his magnificent mansion is the Circular Hall, which features a fine ceiling painting, *The Triumph of Venus*, and remarkable *trompe l'oeil* murals. Durasov hosted balls and banquets in the neighbouring Marble Hall. ◈ *Map B2 • Ulitsa Letnya 1 • (495) 350 1553 • Metro: Volga • Open 7am–6pm Tue–Sun • Adm*

8 Novospasskiy Monastery

Founded within the Kremlin in the 14th century, Novospasskiy Monastery was relocated to its current position, on the bank of the Moskva river, in 1491, on the orders of Ivan the Great (1440–1505). There it formed part of the city's southern defences. The monastery's walls were erected in the 17th century when the Romanov family adopted the pretty Transfiguration Cathedral

The Battle of Borodino

Russian troops met Napoleon's army in Borodino on 7 September 1812. Both sides suffered major casualties during the battle, which culminated with the strategic withdrawal of Russian troops. By burning much of Moscow as they retreated, the Russians left their enemies without supplies as winter closed in. The French were soon forced to abandon the city.

 The grounds of the Museum of the Great Patriotic War comprise a mosque, church and synagogue honouring victims of the war.

as their burial chapel *(see p37)*. Used as a prison during the Soviet era, the monastery was returned to the Orthodox Church in 1991. ◊ *Map G5 • Krestyanskaya Ploshchad • (495) 676 9570 • Metro: Proletarskaya • Open 7am–7pm*

Moscow State University
On completion in 1953, the university was Europe's tallest building. Its spire rises 240 m (790 ft) and is crowned by an 11,980-kg (13-ton) star ringed by carved ears of wheat. The four massive wings, containing over 6,000 dormitory-style rooms, are adorned by a clock, thermometer and barometer that were once the world's largest. The interior is richly decorated with marble panelling, mosaics and sculptures. ◊ *Map A2 • Universitetskaya Ploshchad • Metro: Vorobyovy Gory • www.msu.ru*

Interior, Tolstoy House Museum

Tolstoy House Museum
Leo Tolstoy spent the winters at this city house from 1882 until 1901. Besides family heirlooms, it contains portraits of the Tolstoy family by leading Russian painters. Upstairs are the writer's study and the parlour in which he entertained visitors. ◊ *Map D5 • Ulitsa Lva Tolstovo 21 • (495) 246 9444 • Metro: Park Kultury • Open 10am–5pm Tue–Sun • Adm*

A Day of Museums and Monuments

Morning

Starting at Pobedy Park metro station, cross under Kutuzovskiy Prospekt and head towards the **Victory Monument** – an obelisk in that marks the location of the **Museum of the Great Patriotic War**. Explore the exhibition and, if there is time, wander through the park. Otherwise, retrace your steps and cross to the other side of Kutuzovskiy Prospekt. Walk past the Triumphal Arch, built to mark Russia's victory over Napoleon and now marooned between traffic lanes. Just beyond is the **Borodino Panorama Museum**, fronted by a statue of General Kutuzov, who led the Russian forces in the Great Patriotic War. Have lunch at **Bocconcino** *(see p99)* in the shopping mall just beyond Park Pobedy metro, before taking a metro ride to VDNKh.

Afternoon

From VDNKh station walk past the magnificent **Monument to the Conquerors of Space** *(see p47)* towards the monumental entrance gates of the **All-Russian Exhibition Centre**. Here, outside the old Space Pavilion, is the star exhibit – a Vostock rocket similar to that used by Yuri Gagarin, the first man in space, to circle the earth in 1961. Explore the exhibition centre or exit the main gates and bear right towards Ulitsa Ostankinskaya and the delightful 18th-century **Ostankino Palace** *(see p98)*. Cross the road to the **Kosmos** hotel *(see p114)*, which contains several good restaurants as well as a ten-lane bowling alley.

Leo Tolstoy wrote The Death of Ivan Illyich *in his study at the Tolstoy House Museum.*

Left **White House** Centre **Ostankino Palace** Right **Cathedral of the Intercession, Izmaylovo Park**

Best of the Rest

1 White House
The House of Government formerly served as the seat of the Soviet parliament. ⊛ *Map C3*
• *Krasnopresnenskaya nab. 2*
• *Metro: Barrikadnaya*

2 World Trade Centre Moscow
World-class business centre built in 1980 and expanded in 2004. ⊛ *Map B3* • *Krasnopresnenskaya nab.* • *Metro: Barrikadnaya* • *www.wtcmoscow.ru*

3 Tsaritsyno Palace
A charming ensemble of imaginative buildings, woods and lakes, left unfinished under Catherine the Great. ⊛ *Map B3* • *Ulitsa Dolskaya 1* • *(495) 322 6843* • *Metro: Tsaritsino* • *Open 11am–6pm Wed–Sun* • *Adm* • *www.tsaritsyno.net*

4 Dostoevsky House Museum
Fyodor Dostoevsky's *(see p42)* home contains the writer's manuscripts and quill pen. ⊛ *Map E1* • *Ulitsa Dostoevskovo 2* • *(495) 281 1085* • *Metro: Novoslobodskaya* • *Open 2–8pm Wed, Fri; 10am–6pm Thu, Sat–Sun* • *Adm*

5 Ostankino Palace
This remarkable feat of serf craftsmanship was built for Nikolai Sheremetev in 1797. ⊛ *Map A1* • *Ulitsa Ostankinskaya* • *(495) 683 4645* • *Metro: VDNKh* • *Open May–Sept: 11am–7pm Wed–Sun* • *Adm*

6 Spasso-Andronikov Monastery
Many of the glorious frescoes here are by Andrey Rublev *(see p22)*. A museum dedicated to his art is housed within the complex. ⊛ *Map H4* • *Andronevskaya Ploshchad* • *(495) 678 1467* • *Metro: Ploshchad Ilyicha* • *Open 11am–6pm* • *Adm*

7 Simonov Monastery
This 1370 monastic stronghold was all but demolished under Communism; a church and parts of the ancient walls remain. ⊛ *Map B2* • *Ulitsa Vostochnaya* • *Metro: Avtozavodskaya* • *Open 10am–6pm*

8 Izmaylovo Park
The 1679 Cathedral of the Intercession is just one of the attractions here. ⊛ *Map B2* • *Narodny Prospekt 17* • *Metro: Izmaylovskiy Park*

9 Svyato Donskoy Monastery
One of the fortified monasteries that formed the city's southern defence ring, this 16th-century complex was founded by Boris Gudunov. ⊛ *Map A2* • *Ulitsa Donskoya* • *Metro: Shabolovskaya* • *Open 10am–7pm*

10 Danilovskiy Monastery
Moscow's oldest monastery was founded in 1282 by Grand Prince Daniil. ⊛ *Map B2* • *Danilovskiy val* • *Metro: Tulskaya* • *Open 7am–7pm*

Danilovskiy Monastery's 18 bells were recently returned to it, having been kept at Harvard University, USA, during Communism.

Price Categories

For a three-course meal for one with half a bottle of house wine (or equivalent meal).

R	Under 800 Rub
RR	800–1,500 Rub
RRR	1,500–2,000 Rub
RRRR	2,000–2,500 Rub
RRRRR	Over 2,500 Rub

Interior of Yar restaurant

🔟 Bars and Restaurants

1 Yar
Established in 1826, Yar serves a mixture of French and Russian cuisine in grand surroundings. 🚫 *Map A2 • Sovietsky Hotel, Leningradskiy proezd 32/2 • (495) 960 2004 • Metro: Dinamo • RRRRR*

2 Pinocchio
This chic 1930s-style Italian restaurant has lovely retro furniture and its classic pizzas are among the best in town. 🚫 *Map C4 • Kutuzovskiy proezd 4/2 • (495) 545 0171 • Metro: Kievskaya • RRRRR*

3 Darbar
Darbar offers an excellent selection of Indian dishes and superb views from its 16th-floor position. 🚫 *Map A2 • Sputnik Hotel, Leningradskiy proezd 38 • (495) 930 2925 • Metro: Leninskiy Prospekt • RRR*

4 Grabli
Grabli is a chain of stylish self-service restaurants serving high-quality Russian and international cuisine. A great place to sample classics such as *blini* (pancakes). 🚫 *Map C4 • Kievskaya Ploshchad 2 • (495) 229 1977 • Metro: Kievskaya • RR*

5 Bocconcino
This well-established chain of pizzerias offers an excellent range of Italian dishes. 🚫 *Map A2 • Kutuzovskiy Prospekt 48 • (495) 662 1135 • Metro: Park Pobedy • RRR*

6 Krambambulya
Named after a Belarusian liquor, Krambambulya serves a good range of Belarusian dishes, with many potato-based options. 🚫 *Map B1 • All-Russian Exhibition Centre, Bldg 352 • (499) 760 2307 • Metro: VDNKh • RR*

7 The Apartment
Here you can expect stylish decor and top-notch cuisine. 🚫 *Map C5 • Savvinskaya nab. 21 • (495) 518 6060 • Metro: Kievskaya • RRRR*

8 Vinnaya Istoria
An astounding 140-page wine list and helpful sommeliers are the main draws at this elegant restaurant. 🚫 *Map A1 • Ulitsa Tikhvinskaya 17/1 • (499) 978 9885 • Metro: Savelovskaya, Novoslobodskaya • RRRR*

9 Soup Café
This laid-back café serves mostly Russian dishes with an emphasis on delicious soups. 🚫 *Map A1 • Ulitsa 1st Brestskaya 62/25 • (495) 251 1383 • Metro: Beloruskaya • RR*

10 Sky Lounge
Creative cuisine and fine views from the 22nd floor are the main attractions at this bar-restaurant. 🚫 *Map A2 • Russian Academy of Sciences, Leninskiy Prospekt 32a • (495) 938 5775 • Metro: Leninskiy Prospekt • RRRRR*

Yar restaurant puts on regular shows featuring traditional music and dancing.

STREETSMART

MOSCOW'S TOP 10

Left **The French Embassy, housed in Igumnov House** Right **A sign for a currency exchange office**

🔟 Planning Your Visit

1 When to Go
Moscow has mild summers and cold, but often sunny, winters. The best time to visit is from June to September, when temperatures rise to around 18°C (64°F). They drop to an average of -7°C (44°F) between December and March.

2 What to Pack
Bring plenty of layers in winter, such as thermal leggings and gloves, a warm hat, and waterproof footwear. An anorak or umbrella will do for spring and autumn showers. A T-shirt and shorts are good for summer, although you may need long sleeves and trousers to enter some churches and monasteries.

3 Visas and Passports
Most nationalities need a visa for Russia. To obtain a 30-day tourist visa, submit a passport valid for at least six months after the date of entry, a visa application form, the fee, a passport photograph, and two separate documents – a tourist voucher and an invitation letter provided by your hotel or travel agent.

4 Registration
All visitors to Russia must register with the police within 72 hours of arrival. Your hotel or hostel is legally obliged to register you within 24 hours of your arrival and

may charge a fee for this. Those staying in private homes must be registered by their hosts.

5 Customs
Russian customs regulations are notoriously strict. Anyone bringing cash worth over 337,520 Rub (€7,360) or valuable items into Russia should ensure that they declare them on a stamped customs declaration form, which must be produced upon departure. Any antiques exported from Russia need certification to prove they have no cultural or historical value.

6 Embassies and Consulates
For advice on visa re-quirements, contact your nearest Russian embassy or consulate. Note that the Russian Consulate in London has outsourced its visa service to M/S VF Services (http://ru. vfsglobal.co.uk). Many countries, including the US, UK and several European countries, have embassies in Moscow.

7 Money
Russia's currency – the rouble – can only be purchased within Russia. Euros, US dollars and pounds sterling are the most easily exchangeable currencies *(see p109)*.

8 Time Zone
Moscow is three to four hours ahead of GMT, eight hours ahead of US

Eastern Standard Time, and six hours behind Australian Eastern Standard time.

9 Electrical Appliances
Russia uses 220 V-style twin-pin sockets that are compatible with most European plugs. If you are carrying appliances that have British or American plugs, remember to bring adaptors, as these are hard to find in Moscow. They can usually be bought at airports.

10 Language
The main challenge for most beginners in Russian is the Cyrillic alphabet. Those planning to spend more than a few days in Moscow should consider learning it, as street signs, metro station information boards and bus timetables are all written in Cyrillic. Try to learn a few basic phrases – few Russians speak English well.

Directory

Russian Embassies/ Consulates Abroad
• *London: 5 Kensington Palace Gardens; +44 20 3051 1199; www. rusemblon.org*

• *New York: 9 East 91st St; +1 212 348 0926; www.ruscon.com*

• *Canberra: 78 Canberra Ave, Griffith; +61 2 6295 9474; www.australia. mid.ru*

Left **Boat on the Moskva river** Right **Arbatskaya metro station**

Getting There and Around

Airports
Sheremetevo 2, the oldest of Moscow's three main international airports, is located north of the city, and is linked to Savelovskaya metro station by an express train. The newer Vnukovo Airport, in the southeast, has an express train connection to Kievskaya metro station, and Domodedovo Airport, in the southwest, is linked to Paveletskaya metro station.

Train Stations
Passengers from western Europe arrive at Belorusskiy Station (Belorusskaya metro). Those travelling from Prague, Budapest and Kiev arrive at Kievskiy Station (Kievskaya metro). Arrivals from St Petersburg disembark at Leningradskiy Station, one of three main stations on Komsomolskay Ploshchad (Komsomolskaya metro).

Bus Stations
Eurolines buses arrive at Leningradskiy Station, while buses to and from St Petersburg and all other Russian cities operate from the Central Bus Station, which, it should be noted, is nowhere near the city centre. ⓢ *Leningradskiy Station: Map H1; 3 Komsomolskaya Ploshchad; Komsomolskaya (metro) • Central Bus Station: Map B1; Ulitsa Uralskaya 2; Shchyolskaya (metro)*

River Station
The Northern River Terminal on the outskirts of Moscow is the usual docking and departure point for boats serving St Petersburg.
ⓢ *Northern River Terminal: Map A1 • Leningradskoye shosse 51 • (495) 457 4050 • Rechnoy Vokzal (metro)*

Metro
Moscow's metro system *(see pp24–5)*, which handles more passengers than the London and New York subways combined, is by far the easiest way to get around the city. Passengers can buy single tickets or multiple-journey cards that are swiped upon entry and valid for the length of the journey.

Taxis
Moscow has official, metered taxis identifiable by their chequered doors, but Russians usually prefer to flag down any car and negotiate a fare with the driver. Single female travellers should opt for Pink Taxi or Ladies Red Taxi, both of which are considered to be safe. ⓢ *Ladies Red Taxi: (495) 646 0846 • New Moscow Taxi: (495) 780 6780 • New Yellow Taxi: (495) 940 8888 • Pink Taxi: (495) 662 0003*

Buses, Trams and Trolleybuses
An extensive network of buses, trams, and trolleybuses covers Moscow, operating from 6am to 1am the next morning. Tickets are available at kiosks next to stops or from the driver and are valid for a single journey.

Minibuses
Private minibuses, or *marshrutki*, follow numbered routes with destinations pasted on their windows. Although these are slightly more expensive than public transport, they are much quicker and can be flagged down at any point along their route.

Car Rental and Driving
Europcar has car rental offices at Moscow's three international airports as well as in town. Thrifty has a central rental office on Leningradskoe shosse. Drivers must carry their passport, car registration documents and driving licence, and ensure that the car is equipped with a fire extinguisher, first-aid kit and fluorescent jacket. Cautious driving is advisable. ⓢ *Europcar: (495) 783 7161 • Thrifty Car Rental: (495) 788 6888*

Walking
The central sights around Red Square and the Kremlin can easily be covered on foot, as can the churches and galleries of the Zamoskvoreche district. Wear comfortable shoes.

For details on agencies that assist with visa applications, visit **www.russianvisa.net**

Left **Raising a toast** Centre **A woman leaving church** Right **A doorman outside a restaurant**

Etiquette

Greetings
Men greet each other with a handshake. Women are greeted with a nod or, if they are very close, a kiss on the cheek. Friends of all ages greet each other with the word *"privet,"* while *"zdravstvuyte"* is used for formal occasions.

Political Discussions
Russians are, more by circumstance than by desire, accustomed to political discussion. While the younger generation is more politically apathetic than that which grew up in the USSR, discussions on topics such as the Chechen War can become heated, particularly if a tone critical of Russia's actions there is taken.

Personal Questions
Russians are a lot more willing to ask, and answer, questions that in the West might be considered to be of a personal nature. You might be asked about your salary, or even your family life. However, as a foreigner, you could be seen to be "prying" if you were the one to initiate such questions.

Giving Up Seats
It is accepted practice for young passengers on public transport to give up seats to their elders, pregnant women and people with disabilities.

Failure to do so may lead to on-the-spot public condemnation from your fellow passengers. The younger generation is, however, slowly losing the habit of public transport gallantry.

Male–Female Relations
Men are expected to foot the bill for their female companions in restaurants. Any suggestion to split the cost would be frowned upon. It is also common for women to find doors opened for them, to be helped off buses and to be excluded from any physical work.

Drinking Customs
Russians drink plenty of vodka and the process of drinking has its own rituals. Never drink from the bottle and always take a bite to eat between shots. Toasts are long and frequently made; if you are called upon to make one, a simple *"Za zdorovie!"* ("To your health!") may not be enough.

Smokers
Russians are among the world's heaviest smokers. Most restaurants have a smoking section and there are no smoke-free bars or clubs. However, smoking is banned on public transport. Cigarettes are cheap, with many foreign brands being bootlegged. Non-filtered

cigarettes, manufactured in Russia and sold for absurdly cheap prices, are also available.

Being a Guest
If you are invited to a private flat, it is customary to bring a bottle of alcohol and some flowers for the woman of the house. Russians take their shoes off at home and change into slippers.

The "Public Front"
In offices, shops and stations, there is a "public front" which translates into a certain rudeness when dealing with strangers, although attitudes are changing. These same people may well be warm, kind individuals at heart, but if you encounter them in their guise of minor official, shop assistant or ticket-seller, you are not likely to experience the benign side of their character.

In Churches
Orthodox churches are intense places where mankind is made to feel utterly humble. There are no pews; worshippers stand for the duration of the services. Women cover their heads while men remove their hats. Photography may be strictly forbidden in some churches, but is allowed for a fee in others. Candles, usually sold on the spot, can be placed in front of the icons.

Left **Visitors on a bus tour** Right *The Moscow Times* on a café table

Sources of Information

Websites
The websites of *The Moscow Times* and *In Your Pocket Moscow* provide cultural events listings and travel information, while the *Moscow Info* and *Moscow Taxi* websites offer a good range of general information. The UK Foreign Office website provides useful up-to-date security, health and travel advice.

Newspapers and Magazines in English
The Moscow Times and the *Moscow News* are weekly newspapers, while *In Your Pocket Moscow* is a useful monthly guide. All three are distributed for free in bars, restaurants and hotels. *Passport Moscow* is a monthly lifestyle magazine. 🌐 *www. moscowtimes.com • www.mnweekly.ru • www. inyourpocket.com • www. passportmagazine.com*

Foreign-Language Radio
The Voice of Russia radio station broadcasts a wide range of programmes in many languages. Its website lists schedules and radio frequencies and has an audio archive. The BBC World Service currently broadcasts in Russia twice a day on long wave radio.
🌐 *www.ruvr.ru • www.bbc. co.uk/worldservice*

Business Information
Moscow's World Trade Centre posts a variety of business-related articles on its website and both *The Moscow Times* and *Moscow News* have business news sections. The British and US embassies in Moscow issue monthly economics reports via their websites.
🌐 *www.wtc.ru • www. ukinrussia.fco.gov.uk • http:// moscow.usembassy.gov*

Maps
Most hotels will provide simple maps of the city centre. Try bookshops for detailed maps and street directories of Moscow and beyond. Many maps are printed in the Cyrillic alphabet, but some bilingual versions are also available.

Travel Agencies
Talarii Travel offers a wide range of travel services. Those interested in eco-tourism should try the Dersu Uzala Agency.
🌐 *Talarii Travel: Map C3; Ulitsa Novyy Arbat 36/9; (495) 690 9563; www.talarii. ru • Dersu Uzala Agency: Map L3; 1st Tschemilovskiy pereulok, Bldg 1; (495) 518 5968; www.ecotours.ru*

Gay Visitors
Homosexuality is still frowned upon in Russia, but gay-rights activists continue their campaigns. The website Gay Russia features a gay-focused guide and downloadable "gay map" of Moscow.
🌐 *www.gayrussia.ru*

Disabled Visitors
Moscow's disabled facilities have long been inadequate, but there are signs of improvement. New public buildings, offices and hotels are being fitted with ramps and lifts. The metro system remains inaccessible to wheelchairs.

City Tours
Both Capital Tours and Patriarshy Dom Tours run daily bus tours of the city, but those run by the latter are particularly good. In summer, ferries run a regular service between river stations.
🌐 *Capital Tours: Map N3; Gostiny Dvor Bldg, Ulitsa Ilyinka 4, entrance 6; (495) 232 2442; www.capitaltours. ru • Patriarshy Dom Tours: Map J2; Vspolny pereulok 6; (495) 795 0927; www. russiatravel-pdtours. netfirms.com*

Cultural Centres
The American Cultural Centre, a library and information centre, organizes regular events. The Grint Centre runs Russian language and culture courses.
🌐 *American Cultural Centre: Map Q4; Library for Foreign Literature, Ulitsa Nikoloyanskaya 1; (495) 777 6530; http://amc.ru • Grint Centre: Map B2; Ulitsa Yunosty 5/1, Bldg 6; (495) 374 7430; www.grint.ru*

> *The Russian organization Perspektiva offers current information on disability issues online at http://eng.perspektiva-inva.ru/*

Left **Paintings on sale, Ulitsa Arbat** Right **GUM shopping centre**

🔟 Shopping Tips

Opening Hours
The main opening hours for most shops are Monday to Saturday from 9am until 6pm. Larger shops and malls tend to open at around 10 or 11am and close between 10 and 11pm. Small shops usually close for an hour at lunchtime.

DVDs and CDs
Although you'll still come across the odd rickety street stall piled with cheap pirated CDs and DVDs, gone are the days when regular shops sold them alongside the much more expensive original copies. Nowadays, Mir Kino is one of the best stocked DVD stores in Moscow.
- 🖎 Mir Kino: Map P2
- • Ulitsa Maroseyka 6/8
- • (495) 628 5145

Refunds
Refunds are hard to get in Moscow, as shops generally don't consider themselves responsible for the quality of the items they sell and tend to point unsatisfied customers in the direction of the producer. You may have better luck with small craft and souvenir shops, but they are more likely to offer an exchange than a refund.

Electrical Goods
Although all the usual electronic goods are available in Moscow, there is no particular reason to buy them here, as prices are much the same as in other European countries.

Designer Labels
The boutiques along Ultisa Petrovka and in the Petrovskiy Pasazh, TsUM (see p86) and GUM (see p64) shopping malls are just some of the many outlets that sell high-end designer goods at extortionate prices – often outstripping those in London, Paris and Milan. Those seeking value for money should stick to window-shopping.

Buying Antiques
There are strict customs regulations governing the export of antiques. Paintings, icons and antiques over 100 years old require an export licence, usually procured at great cost and loss of time. Printed material produced before 1958 needs an "expert's certificate", which can be obtained from certain accredited shops.

Sales
Moscow's shops have seasonal sales in the same way as most other cities. However, considering the extortionate prices of some of the designer-label clothes they sell, it may seem that even with a 50 per cent discount you will not be getting much of a bargain.

Haggling
Unless they are having a slow day, the market traders running souvenir stalls around Red Square are unlikely to haggle over prices. It can be quite different at Izmaylovo market (see p52), where most traders seem willing to negotiate. Resist haggling before you have checked the prices of similar goods at neighbouring stalls.

Kassa System
The Kassa system is an exasperating product of Communism that has thankfully nearly died out. It required shop customers to queue two or three times in order to purchase a single item. In the first queue customers received a ticket stating the price of their item; in the second they paid for it and received another ticket; in the third queue they got to exchange the ticket for the item.

Bargains
Izmaylovo market (see p52) is by far the best place to hunt for bargains. Besides the hand-painted icons sold in churches and monasteries, it sells a wide variety of souvenirs as well as rugs and general bric-à-brac. Smokers will be delighted that cigarettes cost as little as 45 Rub (€1) a packet.

Left **Church of the Trinity in Nikitniki** Centre **A city bus** Right **A busy park in autumn**

TOP 10 Moscow on a Budget

1 Free Wi-Fi
Those with laptops can take advantage of the free Wi-Fi access provided by most cafés, bars and hotels, although a few establishments charge by the hour. Some McDonalds restaurants offer customers free use of computers with Internet access.

2 Hostels and Homestays
Hostels offer the cheapest accommodation in Moscow, starting at around 675 Rub (€15) per night for a dormitory bed and 1,345 Rub (€30) for a twin room. Dorms are mixed-sex and reasonably clean. Homestays are also an inexpensive option, but are only usually available to those enrolled on Russian language courses. ✎ www.hofa.ru

3 Parks
There are plenty of huge parks (see p45) to visit in Moscow. Gorky is the most central and has a funfair; Izmaylovo is one of the largest; and Kolomenskoe is a picturesque spot with a historic estate. In winter, Moscow's ponds and lakes turn into ice rinks that anyone with a pair of skates can enjoy.

4 Business Lunches/Buffets
Business lunches are a great way to save money in this costly city. Most restaurants offer a set

menu of a non-alcoholic drink, starter, main course and dessert for a fixed price between noon and 4pm on weekdays. Another money saver is the all-you-can-eat buffet, where you "buy" a plate and fill it as many times as you can. Shesh Besh (see p93) has a very good all-you-can-eat salad bar.

5 City Transport
For less than 44 Rub (€1) you can catch a bus, tram or trolley bus and cross the entire city. One of the best bus routes is No. 119, which starts at Kievskaya metro station and takes passengers to the giant Moscow State University building (see p97). Trolleybus No. 7 begins at Park Pobedy metro and travels all the way to Kamenny Most, beside the Kremlin.

6 Student Discounts
Holders of international student cards are entitled to a 50 per cent discount at all state museums and galleries. Those with student cards issued in Russia pay even less. Students can also benefit from discounts on train fares, pubic transport passes, and concert and theatre tickets.

7 Churches
Although Stalin destroyed an estimated 400 of Moscow's historic

churches, plenty remain scattered throughout the city and they are all free to enter. The only exception is St Basil's Cathedral (see pp8–9).

8 Metro Sightseeing
It is possible to spend an entire day exploring the magnificent stations of Moscow's metro system (see pp24–5) for the price of a ticket. Construction began in the 1930s and is still underway today as the system expands further into the suburbs.

9 Food Stalls
Food stalls and markets are the cheapest and quickest way to eat when you are out and about. Tempting options include fresh blini (pancakes), hot dogs, Chinese noodles and pirogi (pies). It is best to avoid the kebab stalls, as they have notoriously low hygiene standards.

10 Window Shopping
Moscow is packed with window-shopping opportunities. These range from elegant boutiques in splendid malls, such as GUM (see p64) and TsUM (see p86), which stock the world's most exclusive labels, to mainstream malls and the bustling markets at Dorogomilovskiy and Izmaylovo (see p52).

Left **A pharmacy exterior** Centre **Police car** Right **Fire engine**

Health and Security

1 Personal Safety

Keep credit cards and most of your cash in a hidden money belt while carrying a small sum in your pocket or wallet that can be handed over if necessary. Carry a photocopy of your passport rather than the original, avoid walking alone late at night and watch out for scams (see p110).

2 Women Travelling Alone

Although single Russian women can often be spotted flagging down taxis, it is not advisable for female tourists to do the same. The women-only taxi service provided by Pink Taxi and Ladies Red Taxi are highly recommended (see p103). Unaccompanied women should also exercise caution entering nightclubs as they may be mistaken for prostitutes and hassled by doormen.

3 Emergency Services

Police, fire and ambulance services can be contacted using emergency numbers (fire: 01; police: 02; ambulance: 03). Operators are unlikely to understand foreign languages, so it is advisable, if at all possible, to engage the help of a Russian speaker.

4 Police

Moscow's police are best avoided unless you are in genuine trouble,

when a loud shout or scream should hopefully bring them running.

5 Theft

Moscow's violent crime rate is low compared with other major capitals, but petty theft is rife and visitors should be constantly vigilant against pickpockets (see p110). Store valuables in the hotel safe and keep your camera and wallet well out of sight.

6 Terrorism

The late 1990s and early 2000s saw a number of bombings and attacks on Moscow, including the Dubrovka Theatre Siege in 2002 (see p33), as Chechen separatists strove to establish an independent state. However, the end of the Chechen War has seen the terrorist threat decrease significantly in recent years.

7 Health Precautions

Visitors should stick to bottled mineral water or boil their tap water before drinking. Food poisoning is a common complaint which can be avoided to some extent by frequent hand washing. Check with your doctor about vaccinations before departing.

8 Medical Treatment

Russian hospitals will provide free basic treatment for most foreign visitors, but the standard

of care is likely to be lower than in their home country. Visitors should ensure they have a good medical insurance policy allowing them to use the city's expensive private medical clinics, which have higher standards.
§ American Clinic: Map G1; Grokholskiy pereulok 31; (495) 937 5757 • European Medical Centre: Map K2; Spiriodonevskiy pereulok 5; (495) 933 6655

9 Pharmacies

Apteka (pharmacies) are identifiable by a green cross hanging outside, and stock a wide range of products and medicines. However, visitors on prescription medication should take the precaution of carrying with them enough to cover their trip. Branches of the 24-hour pharmacy chain 36.6 can be found throughout the city, including some in the city centre. Taxi drivers should also be able to help locate them.
§ Map D2: Ulitsa 1st Tverskaya-Yamskaya 8/1 • Map K4: Novyy Arbat 15 • Map R2: Zemlyanoy val 25

10 Insurance

Medical insurance is compulsory for tourists visiting Russia. When choosing a policy it may be worth opting for a provider that will pay for any treatment on the spot instead of reimbursing the costs upon your return home.

Streetsmart

Left **A post office sign** Centre **An Internet café** Right **An ATM**

🔟 Banking and Communications

Currency
Russia's currency is the rouble (Rub) which is split into 100 kopeks. Though the rouble stabilized following the 1998 financial crisis, it has been severely weakened by the 2008–9 global credit crisis. Russian roubles are not sold outside Russia, so visitors must purchase them upon arrival.

Credit Cards
Although credit cards are accepted at most major restaurants, hotels and supermarkets, many smaller establishments are not equipped to deal with them, so always carry cash as a back-up. Keep a photocopy of your cards separately and warn your card providers that you will be travelling abroad to prevent your cards from being automatically blocked for security reasons.

ATMs
ATMs are as ubiquitous here as in any other major city and most offer currency withdrawal in roubles, dollars and euros. Try to avoid using machines that are not attached to banks; staff in shops and bars with ATMs will not have access to the machines in the event of your card being swallowed.

Changing Money
Numerous small exchange bureaus can be found in kiosks around the city centre. Most are commission-free, but check the rates before proceeding to ensure you get a fair deal. Banks and hotels are the safest places to change money, but usually charge quite high commission fees.

Traveller's Cheques
The Bank of Moscow will change American Express traveller's cheques commission-free, while most other banks charge around 3 per cent. Some larger hotels can also change traveller's cheques for a sizeable commission.
🏦 Bank of Moscow: Map M1 • Ulitsa Tverskaya 8 • (495) 299 2010

International Money Transfers
International money transfers can be received via Western Union at most Russian banks. Transfers can be completed in a few minutes and are paid out in US dollars. Recipients must produce a valid form of identification.
🏦 www.westernunion.ru

Telephones and Dialling Codes
Public telephones can be found all over the city. Some accept coins, but most require phone cards that can be purchased in metro stations, banks, post offices, and some newspaper kiosks. The city code 495 covers most of Moscow, but some parts of the city use 499. When calling between cities in Russia, dial 8 followed by the city code and the local number. To phone abroad, dial 8 followed by 10 and then the country code.

Mobile Phones
Mobile phones with roaming will function normally in Russia, but making and receiving calls is very expensive. Check prices with your phone provider before your departure and consider buying a Russian SIM card to use for the duration of your stay.

Internet Access
Moscow is well-equipped for anyone with a laptop, as almost every hotel, bar and café has a Wi-Fi connection. Most are free, though a few charge by the hour. There are plenty of Internet clubs in Moscow. One of the most central is the 24-hour TimeOnline Internet Club in the Manezh Mall (see p86).

Post
The Russian postal service is notoriously slow; international post is likely to take between two and four weeks to arrive at its destination. DHL has an office in the Marriott Grand Hotel.
🏦 Main Post Office: Map P1; Ulitsa Myasnitskaya 26/2 • DHL: Map E2; Ulitsa Tverskaya 26; (495) 956 1000; www.dhl.ru

Left **Flagging down a taxi** Centre **A policeman checking documents** Right **Rank of unofficial taxis**

Things to Avoid

1 Police
There is a heavy police presence in Moscow, but the usual wisdom applies – if you have done nothing wrong, they are unlikely to be a problem. In case you are stopped, it is advisable to carry a photocopy of your passport and visa to show them rather than handing over your original documents.

2 Scams
An enormous variety of scams have been practised at one time or another in Moscow. A recurring favourite is for a passerby to drop a wallet bulging with cash as he passes you; picking it up will lead you into trouble. You should also avoid any foreigners apparently in distress who claim to need your help urgently. In general, exercise extreme caution when approached by strangers.

3 Street Money Changers
Never change money on the street, even if you have been offered a great exchange rate; it is likely that you will be cheated or robbed by getting involved with street hustlers. Stick to banks, hotels, or exchange kiosks.

4 Standing Out
It may sound obvious, but the more you can blend into the crowd, the better. Avoid speaking too loudly in a foreign language or wandering around with your nose buried in a map or guide book. One of the best ways to avoid attention is to buy a Russian newspaper and carry it tucked under your arm.

5 Offers of Cheap Rooms
Private adverts offering unbelievably cheap rooms in the city centre can often be seen plastered on walls in public areas. Avoid being drawn in by such apparent bargains, as sooner or later it will transpire that the prices are accompanied by extortionate agency fees.

6 Taxis without an Agreed Fare
All official taxis in Moscow have meters (see p103), but some are so out-of-date that the driver will prefer to negotiate the fare with the passenger. Always agree on the fare before accepting the ride to avoid the driver naming an exorbitant price at your destination.

7 Taxi Drivers on Foot
Avoid taxi drivers who approach you on foot offering transport in their nearby vehicle. This often happens outside restaurants, nightclubs, train stations and airports, and is very likely to lead to trouble. Look for the nearest queue of taxis or flag one down and approach it yourself instead.

8 Crowded Areas
Try to avoid large crowds and travelling in overcrowded public transport, especially in the city centre. Pickpockets often target buses and trams, using knives to slice open bags and remove valuables before jumping off at the next stop. Be sure to keep your bag in sight and your valuables out of sight.

9 Street Toilet Cubicles
Lines of portable plastic toilet cubicles are a frequent sight in the centre and are best avoided. A far better option is to walk into a hotel or restaurant and ask to use their facilities, or head for the nearest branch of McDonalds.

10 Crossing the Road
Drivers in Moscow seem to treat ring roads as their own personal racetrack and frequently hurtle by at breakneck speeds. Pedestrian crossings never seem to provide enough time to cross these vast eight-lane highways, often leaving people stranded midway across. It is worth walking further up the road until you find a *perehod* (underpass).

For telephone numbers of safe taxi firms See p103.

Left **Salad served at a vegetarian restaurant** Right **Dining at Ludi Kak Ludi restaurant**

🔟 Accommodation and Dining Tips

1 Tipping
Although it is not compulsory to tip in most restaurants, a 10–15 per cent tip will always be appreciated by waiting staff and should hopefully ensure you receive good service if you intend to return. Restaurants that do have a service charge will list it on the menu and the bill.

2 Travelling with Children
It should not be assumed that restaurants will have highchairs or that hotels will have cots, but Russians are very friendly towards children and are likely to be helpful. The city benefits from a great range of fun and interesting activities for children (see pp54–5).

3 Choosing a Hotel
Moscow has a wide variety of accommodation options ranging from homestays and hostels to high-end hotels. Many of the mid-range hotel options are far from the centre in large Soviet-era blocks, so it is worth checking the transport available.

4 Location
One of the most important factors when choosing a hotel is its proximity to a metro station. Note that the metro closes at 1am, so if you are planning any late nights out, a central hotel might be a wise choice.

5 Reservations
It is well worth booking accommodation in advance to save you traipsing around the city in search of available rooms. Numerous international hotel reservation websites will arrange bookings. A small deposit is usually taken by the website and the balance is paid to the hotel upon arrival (beware of sites that demand the balance up front). Most major hotels have their own websites with reservation options.

6 Room Rates
Room rates are fixed and usually quoted on hotel websites. In the older Soviet-era hotels, renovated rooms are offered to foreigners at a higher rate, so those on a budget might try to secure a cheaper deal in a dingy room with retro Soviet decor. Prices usually include breakfast (the standard of which varies) and tend to drop slightly between July and September.

7 Vegetarian Food
Russian cuisine is predominantly meat-based; even salads often contain meat. However, vegetarians are reasonably well catered for with a good range of salads, soups and side dishes on most menus. Japanese restaurants offer plenty of vegetarian options, as do most pizzerias. More and more vegetarian restaurants are springing up around the city. Jagannath (see p72), with its creative Indian vegetarian dishes, is a great option.

8 Business Lunches
The vast majority of restaurants offer an excellent-value set lunch menu on working weekdays (see p107).

9 Types of Cuisine
Moscow's craze for sushi has led to the opening of hundreds of Japanese restaurants, and sushi appears on the menu of almost every eatery. Fortunately, the city is full of alternatives too. Italian, French and Georgian cuisine have long been popular, as have Uzbek, Indian, Chinese, Vietnamese, Turkish and Lebanese, to a lesser extent. Traditional Russian dishes are as ubiquitous as ever.

10 Smoking
At the time of writing the Russian parliament was considering a smoking ban in public places – an unpopular move, as an estimated 40 per cent of Russian adults are smokers. In the meantime, non-smokers make do with separate seating areas in restaurants.

Left **Trans-Siberian Hostel** Centre **HM Hostel building** Right **Comrade Hostel**

TOP 10 Hostels

1 Moscow Home Hostel
A short walk from the city centre, this well-kept collection of dorms and private rooms offers plenty of bathrooms, free Wi-Fi and tea and coffee. ⊗ Map J6 • 2nd Neopalimovskiy pereulok 1/12 • (495) 778 2445 • Metro: Park Kultury • www.moshostel.com • €

2 Napoleon Hostel
Napoleon has a modern interior with spacious, clean dorm rooms. The communal dining area has a bar, Wi-Fi and computers. Helpful staff are on hand to provide city maps and travel advice. ⊗ Map P2 • Ulitsa Maly Zlatoustinskiy 2, 4th floor • (495) 628 6695 • Metro: Kitay Gorod • www.napoleonhostel.com • €

3 Comrade Hostel
Housed in an immaculately maintained 19th-century apartment block, this hostel boasts stylish modern furnishings. Free Internet access is on offer. ⊗ Map P2 • Ulitsa Maroseyka 11, 3rd floor • (495) 628 3126 • Metro: Kitay Gorod • www.comradehostel.com • €

4 Godzilla's Hostel
Godzilla's has private en-suite rooms as well as twin rooms and dormitory accommodation. It also has modern facilities including three kitchens, plenty of bathrooms, and a washing machine. ⊗ Map E2 • Bolshoy Karetnyy 6, Apt 5, 1st floor • (495) 699 4223 • Metro: Tsvetnoy Bulvar • www.godzillashostel.com • €€

5 Hostel Number One
Though it's not the most atmospheric of hostels, the rooms here are large. Friendly staff run regular city tours and can arrange onward travel. ⊗ Map A1 • Ulitsa Chasovaya 27/12, Room 40, 4th floor • (495) 156 7687 • Metro: Sokol • www.sherstone.ru • €€

6 Yellow Blue Bus Hostel
Situated in an intimate apartment, this cosy hostel offers Internet access, a kitchen and a mid-sized communal area. Guests are provided with keys to the building as the hostel is not always staffed 24 hours a day. ⊗ Map D2 • Ulitsa Tverskaya-Yamskaya 5, Apt 8 • (495) 250 1364 • Metro: Mayakovskaya • www.ybbhostel.com • €

7 Trans-Siberian Hostel
Within walking distance of the fashionable Chistye Prudye district, this hostel has double rooms as well as female-only and mixed dorms. Staff can arrange airport transfers and book train and plane tickets. ⊗ Map R2 • Barashevskiy pereulok 12 • (495) 916 2030 • Metro: Kitay Gorod • www.transsiberianhostel.com • €

8 Sweet Moscow Hostel
Located right in the heart of Moscow's historic district, this place is surrounded by bars, restaurants and cafés. Rooms are kept spotlessly clean and guests can enjoy free tea, coffee and Russian biscuits. ⊗ Map J4 • Ulitsa Arbat 51, Apt 31 • (495) 420 3446 • Metro: Smolenskaya • www.sweetmoscow.com • €

9 Home From Home Hostel
The owners have made a real effort to retain the style of this 19th-century apartment by stripping the plaster off the walls and exposing the original wooden window and door frames. It is an appealing, laid-back spot and enjoys an enviable central location. ⊗ Map J4 • Ulitsa Arbat • (495) 229 8018 • Metro: Smolenskaya • www.home-fromhome.com • €€

10 HM Hostel
Situated opposite a pleasant park, this delightful hostel combines high ceilings and period features with modern furnishings. Female-only and mixed dorms are on offer along with kitchen facilities, a lounge area and computers with free Internet access. ⊗ Map K4 • Gogolyevskiy Bulvar 13, Apt 14 • (495) 691 8390 • Metro: Arbatskaya • www.hostel-moscow.com • €

To experience life in a real Russian home, you can arrange to stay with a local family through the Hostel Number One website.

Price Categories

For a standard, double room per night, including taxes and extra charges.

€ Under €60
€€ €60–€120
€€€ €120–€200
€€€€ €200–€300
€€€€€ Over €300

Left **Apartment, Uncle Pasha** Right **Kita Inn Bed & Breakfast**

🔟 Agencies, B&Bs and Flats

1 Samovar Bed & Breakfast

One of Moscow's few B&B-style establishments, this charming place is furnished with a quirky mixture of Soviet-era and modern furniture. Rooms are adorned with paintings and sculptures by local artists. 🚫 Map E2 • Ulitsa Staropimenovskiy pereulok 16, Apt 54 • (495) 772 4002 • Metro: Mayakovskaya • www.samovarmoscow.com • €€€

2 Kita Inn Bed & Breakfast

Enjoying a central location, this B&B overlooks a leafy courtyard. It is comfortably furnished and the breakfast is generous. 🚫 Map D2 • Ulitsa Yamskaya-Tverskaya 2, Bldg 6/7, Entrance 5, Apt 9 • (092) 6664 4118 • Metro: Mayakovskaya • www.kitainn.com • €€

3 Uncle Pasha

Uncle Pasha is an enormously helpful character who runs a website offering information for visitors to Moscow. He also rents out his own centrally located flat, equipped with modern amenities. 🚫 Map P5 • Ovchinnikovskaya nab. 8, kv. 508 • (910) 932 5546 • www.unclepasha.com • €€

4 Moscow Apartments

With a wide range of flats all over the city, Moscow Apartments offers discounts for longer stays. All flats are smartly furnished and have high-speed Internet access and cable television. Bookings can be made by phone or via its website and require a 15 per cent deposit. 🚫 (495) 662 8753 • www.moscow-apartments.net • €€–€€€€

5 Arenda

Though not furnished to the highest standards, Arenda's apartments are kept scrupulously clean and are all conveniently located. 🚫 (926) 236 4545 • www.arenda2000.ru • €€

6 Rick's Apartments

Run by an affable American expatriate resident in Moscow since 1996, Rick's Apartments are all centrally located and comfortably furnished. Most come with a computer and Internet connection as well as a washing machine. Rick will arrange visas for his guests and ensure that they are registered upon arrival. 🚫 (495) 741 7606 • www.enjoymoscow.com • €€–€€€€

7 Astor Apartments

Run by a German company, Astor Apartments has a broad variety of flats priced according to size, location and standard. All are equipped with Internet access, cable television, a kitchen and washing machine. Bookings should be made by phone or via the website. 🚫 (495) 228 1475 • www.astor-apartments.com • €€–€€€€

8 Welcome to Russia

The flats provided by Welcome to Russia are clean and comfortably appointed; some can sleep up to seven people. Bookings are best made via their website. 🚫 (495) 937 4685 • www.welcome-to-russia.com • €€–€€€€

9 Apartments Moscow

Aimed at the upper end of the market, these apartments are furnished to a high standard; some include mock antique furniture and polished wood floors. All are centrally located. 🚫 Map A2 • Leninskiy Prospekt 29, suites 401–408 • (495) 956 4422 • www.apartmentsmoscow.com • €€€

10 Moscow Comfort

This small agency has a selection of six apartments located around the top end of Ulitsa Tverskaya. Clean and simply furnished, the flats are supplied with computers, printers, and Internet access. The owners can help to organize visas and also offer a mobile phone rental service. 🚫 (495) 545 7597 • www.moscow-comfort.com • €€€

Left **Akademicheskaya hotel** Centre **Sputnik hotel** Right **Façade of Zolotoi Kolos hotel**

TOP 10 Mid-Range Soviet-Era Hotels

1 Akademicheskaya
Built in 1972 for guests of the Russian Academy of Sciences, this concrete monolith is reasonably cheap and central. Avoid the rooms that haven't been renovated since 1972. ✆ Map E6 • Ulitsa Donskaya 1 • (495) 959 8157 • Metro: Oktyabrskaya • www.akademicheskaya.ru • €€

2 Sputnik
Another of the city's many Soviet-era blocks, the Sputnik was built in 1968 and underwent complete renovation in 2006. Rooms are small, but the complimentary breakfasts are excellent. Upper-floor rooms offer fine views of Moscow. ✆ Map A2 • Leninskiy Prospekt 38 • (495) 930 2287 • Metro: Leninskiy Prospekt • www.hotelsputnik.ru • €€€

3 Tourist
Set in pleasant surroundings, this sprawling complex of 1950s buildings provides rooms ranging from Economy Standard (not renovated since Soviet times) to Lux Renovated (renovated rooms and bathrooms). ✆ Map B1 • Ulitsa Selkokhozyaystvennaya 17/2 • (495) 737 7910 • Metro: Botanicheskiy Sad • www.hoteltourist.ru • €€€

4 Central Tourist House
Built in 1980, this mighty 33-floor hotel was renovated in 1996 and has a surprisingly smart and modern interior. Facilities include a swimming pool, sauna and fitness centre. Views from the upper floors are breathtaking. ✆ Map A3 • Leninskiy Prospekt 146 • (495) 737 7910 • Metro: Yugo Zapadnaya • www.hotelcdt.ru • €€€

5 Vostok
Located near the All-Russian Exhibition Centre (see p96), the Vostok occupies a small group of buildings surrounded by greenery. Furniture is dated but smart, and staff are helpful. ✆ Map B1 • Ulitsa Gostinichnaya 9a, Bldg 3 • (495) 482 1345 • Metro: Vladykino • www.vostokhotel.ru • €€

6 Zolotoi Kolos
Built in 1954 to coincide with the expansion of the nearby All-Russian Exhibition Centre, this hotel has since been refurbished to a decent standard. Rooms come with mini-bar, fridge and air conditioning. ✆ Map B1 • Ulitsa Yaroslavskaya 15, Bldg 1–8 • (495) 617 6356 • Metro: VDNKh • www.zkolos.ru • €€

7 Universitetskaya
This concrete hotel is in a quiet residential area. Rooms are kept clean, and those that haven't been refurbished for some time are available at bargain prices. The nearest metro station is too far to walk, so guests must take a taxi or use a bus. ✆ Map A2 • Michurinskiy Prospekt 8/29 • (495) 939 9215 • Metro: Universitetskaya • €€–€€€

8 Izmaylovo
Built in 1979 to accommodate athletes for the 1980 Olympics, this group of four huge skyscrapers can accommodate over 10,000 guests. Rooms are simple but cosy. The buildings overlook a lake beside Izmaylovo Park (see p98). ✆ Map B2 • Izmaylovskoe shosse 71 • (495) 737 7910 • Metro: Izmaylovskiy Park • www.hotelizmailovo.ru • €€

9 Kosmos
This crescent-shaped hotel block was designed by French architects in 1979. Most of its 1,777 rooms have been updated to four-star standards. Facilities include a swimming pool, concert hall and bowling alley. ✆ Map B1 • Mira Prospekt 150 • (495) 956 0642 • Metro: VDNKh • www.hotelcosmos-moscow.com • €€€

10 Yunost
Used by Soviet youth organizations and visiting foreign delegations during Communism, the Yunost was built in 1961. The interior is largely Soviet-styled, but renovated rooms are available. ✆ Map C6 • Ulitsa Khamovnicheskiy val 34 • (495) 242 4860 • Metro: Sportivnaya • www.hotelyunost.ru • €€

Price Categories

For a standard, double room per night, including taxes and extra charges.

€	Under €60
€€	€60–€120
€€€	€120–€200
€€€€	€200–€300
€€€€€	Over €300

Library inside the Katerina City hotel

🔟 Business Hotels

1 Belgrad

One of two hotel blocks covered with state-of-the-art neon lights, Belgrad stands opposite the Stalinist Ministry of Foreign Affairs building (see p77). The hotel has a 60-seat conference room and a banquet hall. ◎ Map J5 • Ulitsa Smolenskaya 8 • (499) 248 3125 • Metro: Smolenskaya • www.hotel-belgrad.ru • €€€

2 Budapest

This hotel is in a 19th-century mansion with period features and antique-style furniture. Facilities include a conference room. ◎ Map M1 • Petrovskiy Linii 2/18 • (495) 623 2356 • Metro: Teatralnaya • www.hotel-budapest.ru/main.html • €€€€€

3 Renaissance

This large hotel has over 400 well-furnished rooms, conference facilities, a pool and a fitness centre. The only drawback is its distance from the centre. Guests can use the free shuttle bus to the Kremlin. ◎ Map A1 • Olimpiyskiy Prospekt 18/1 • (495) 777 1938 • Metro: Rizhskaya • www.hotel-renessans.ru • €€€€€

4 Aerostar

Originally planned for the 1980 Olympics, the Aerostar was eventually built in 1989. The bland concrete exterior is as Soviet in appearance as ever, but the interior is a four-star affair aimed at international business travellers. Facilities include 12 conference rooms, a fitness centre and restaurants. ◎ Map A1 • Leningradskiy Prospekt 37, Bldg 9 • (495) 988 3131 • Metro: Dynamo • www.aerostar.ru • €€€€

5 Arbat

Pleasantly located on a quiet backstreet, the Arbat is a lovely modern property just a few minutes' walk from Ulitsa Arbat. Rooms are large and the service is great. The hotel can sleep up to 200 people and has four conference halls. ◎ Map J5 • Plotnikov pereulok 12 • (499) 271 2801 • Metro: Smolenskaya • www.president-hotel.ru • €€€€

6 Proton

Designed with business clients in mind, the Proton is located far from the centre but within easy reach of Moscow's exhibition halls. Room standards are high and the conference facilities excellent. The hotel runs a regular shuttle bus to the nearest metro station. ◎ Map A2 • Ulitsa Novozavodskaya 22 • (495) 797 3300 • Metro: Fili • www.protonhotel.ru • €€€

7 Peking

Built in the Stalinist Gothic architectural style of the 1950s, the Peking offers rooms that have been refurbished to four-star standards as well as some that still belong to the Soviet era. Facilities include a conference room and fitness centre. ◎ Map D2 • Ulitsa Bolshaya Sadovaya 5 • (495) 234 2467 • Metro: Mayakovskaya • www.hotelpekin.ru • €€€€

8 Maxima Slavia

This brand new business hotel provides a conference hall and business centre with state-of-the-art facilities. A regular shuttle bus transports guests to the nearest metro station. ◎ Map B1 • Ulitsa Gostinichnaya 4/9 • (495) 788 7278 • Metro: VDNKh • www.maximahotels.ru • €€

9 Katerina City

A modern business hotel with Scandinavian-style interiors, the Katerina is situated within walking distance of Moscow's business district and ten minutes from the nearest metro station. ◎ Map G5 • Shlyuzovaya nab. 6 • (495) 933 0401 • Metro: Paveletskaya • www.katerina.msk.ru • €€€

10 Iris

The Iris has excellent facilities for business users, but its distance from the centre and lack of a nearby metro station make it an inconvenient choice for regular tourists. The hotel does offer a shuttle bus service from Ulitsa Tverskaya. ◎ Map A1 • Korovinskoe shosse 10 • (495) 933 0533 • www.iris-hotel.ru • €€€€

Recommend your favourite hotel on **traveldk.com**

Left **Lobby at the Golden Apple hotel** Right **Lobby in the Savoy**

🔟 Boutique Hotels

1 Golden Apple
Featuring a huge golden apple in its lobby, this impressive five-star hotel is housed in a fine 19th-century building. The stylish rooms are ultra-modern in design and the deluxe apartments are appointed with Philippe Starck fixtures. ◐ Map E2 • Ulitsa Malaya Dmitrovka 11 • (495) 980 7000 • Metro: Pushkinskaya • www. goldenapple.ru • €€€€

2 Metropol
This renowned Art Nouveau hotel has played host to luminaries throughout modern history, from Tolstoy to Al Gore. Decorated by some of Russia's most famous early 20th-century artists, it is one of Moscow's finest hotels. ◐ Map N2 • Teatralny proezd 1/4 • (499) 501 7800 • Metro: Teatralnaya • www.metropol-moscow.ru • €€€€€

3 Savoy
Refurbished in 2005, this hotel now combines state-of-the-art facilities with lavish 19th-century Neo-Classical style. The Savoy restaurant (see p73) is one of Moscow's best. ◐ Map N2 • Ulitsa Rozhdestvenka 3/6, Bldg 1 • (495) 620 8500 • Metro: Teatralnaya • www.savoy.ru • €€€€€

4 MaMaison Pokrovka
This hotel's refreshing style is a modernized blend of 1930s and 1950s design, with plenty of natural light and motifs borrowed from the Moscow metro. Standards are exceptionally high. ◐ Map R2 • Ulitsa Pokrovka 40/2 • (495) 229 5757 • Metro: Chistye Prudy • www.pokrovka-moscow.com • €€€€

5 Le Royal Meridien National
This grand hotel is one of the city's best and has long been at the centre of historic events. Lenin stayed in room 107 shortly after the 1917 Revolution, and Trotsky made his last speech in Russia from one of its balconies. ◐ Map M3 • Ulitsa Mokhovaya 15/1 • (495) 258 7000 • Metro: Okhotnyy Ryad • www. national.ru • €€€€€

6 East-West
This classy hotel has an intimate atmosphere and a delightful courtyard garden. Its central location puts it within easy walking distance of Moscow's main sights. ◐ Map L2 • Tverskoy Bulvar 14 • (495) 290 0404 • Metro: Pushkinskaya, Arbatskaya • www. eastwesthotel.ru • €€€€€

7 Ritz-Carlton
Ritz-Carlton boasts the largest hotel rooms in town, bathrooms lined with Altai Mountain marble, and views of the Kremlin. Complimentary services on offer include overnight shoe-shining and a personal butler to act as guide and interpreter. ◐ Map M2 • Ulitsa Tverskaya 3 • (495) 225 8888 • Metro: Teatralnaya • www. ritzcarlton.com • €€€€€

8 Sovietsky
This characterful place was added to the exclusive 19th-century Yar restaurant (see p99) by order of Stalin in 1951. Built in Russian Imperial style, it features majestic marble staircases and colonnaded halls. ◐ Map A2 • Leningradskiy proezd 32/2 • (495) 960 2000 • Metro: Leninskiy Prospekt • www.sovietsky.ru • €€€€

9 Swissôtel Krasnye Holmy
Among the city's top contemporary five-star hotels, the 32-floor Swissôtel comes with some of the best views in Moscow. ◐ Map G5 • Kosmodamianskaya nab. 52/6 • (495) 787 9800 • Metro: Paveletskaya • www. swissotel.com • €€€€€

10 Leningradskaya Hilton
Built in the early 1950s, this flagship member of the Hilton chain was recently refurbished to meet international standards of luxury. The building's showpiece is its double-height entrance lobby flanked by a pair of marble staircases. ◐ Map G1 • Ulitsa Kalanchevskaya 21/40 • (495) 627 5550 • Metro: Komsomolskaya • www.hilton.com • €€€€€

Price Categories

For a standard, double room per night, including taxes and extra charges.

€	Under €60
€€	€60–€120
€€€	€120–€200
€€€€	€200–€300
€€€€€	Over €300

Swimming pool at the Ararat Park Hyatt hotel

TOP 10 International Hotels

1 Balchug Kempinski Moscow

Renovated to the exacting standards of the Kempinski chain, this luxurious hotel occupies a 19th-century building that has housed a succession of hotels since 1812. ✪ Map N4 • Ulitsa Balchug 1 • (495) 287 2000 • Metro: Novokuznetskaya • www.kempinski-moscow.com • €€€€€

2 Sheraton Palace

Noted for its reliably high standards and top-class facilities, this hotel has three restaurants serving an excellent variety of cuisine, a fitness centre and a jogging track. ✪ Map D1 • Ulitsa Tverskaya-Yamskaya 1, 19 • (495) 931 9700 • Metro: Belorusskaya • http://eng.sheratonpalace.ru • €€€€

3 Novotel Moscow Centre

Typically smart and functional, the Novotel is characterless and plain, yet comfortingly familiar. Though not particularly central, it is literally on top of a metro station, which makes it an ideal base from which to explore the city. ✪ Map E1 • Ulitsa Novoslobodskaya 23 • (495) 780 4000 • Metro: Mendeleyevskaya • www.novotel.com • €€€

4 Marriott Tverskaya

This vast luxury hotel has an impressive atrium-style central lobby that rises several floors to a glass ceiling. Standards are of the first order, while facilities include five conference rooms, a fitness centre and various business-related services. ✪ Map D1 • Ulitsa 1st Tverskaya-Yamskaya 34 • (495) 258 3000 • Metro: Belorusskaya • www.marriott.com • €€€€

5 Radisson Slavyanskaya

Standing on the banks of the Moskva river, this massive 410-room hotel has some great views of the city. It is also conveniently close to a metro station. ✪ Map C4 • Europe Square 2 • (495) 941 8000 • Metro: Kievskaya • www.moscow.radissonas.com • €€€€€

6 Kebur Palace

This pleasant four-star hotel offers exceptionally good service and standards. It is within walking distance of Gorky Park (see p90) and the New Tretyakov Gallery (see p89) and boasts one of the city's best Georgian restaurants – the Tiflis (see p79). ✪ Map K6 • Ulitsa Ostozhenka 32 • (495) 733 9070 • Metro: Park Kultury • www.hotelkeburpalace.ru • €€€€€

7 Akvarel

Huge gilt-framed mirrors, marble floors and plush antique-style furniture lend the elegant Akvarel plenty of charm, assisted by smartly uniformed staff. ✪ Map M1 • Stoleshnikov pereulok 12 • (495) 502 9430 • Metro: Teatralnaya • www.hotelakvarel.ru • €€€€€

8 Holiday Inn Suschevsky

Reasonably priced for a hotel of this standard, the Holiday Inn is some distance from the centre but near enough to a metro station to allow easy access to the city. Facilities include a fitness centre and a range of business services. ✪ Map A1 • Ulitsa Suschevskiy val 74 • (495) 225 8282 • Metro: Rizhskaya • www.holiday-inn.com • €€€

9 Crowne Plaza

Situated beside the Moskva river, this hotel forms part of World Trade Centre Moscow complex (see p98). A shuttle bus is available to take guests to the closest metro station. ✪ Map C3 • Ulitsa Krasnopresnenskaya 12 • (495) 258 2222 • Metro: Delovoy Tsentr • www.crowneplaza.ru • €€€€

10 Ararat Park Hyatt

This lovely, classy hotel is located right in the centre of Moscow, close to the Bolshoy Theatre (see pp18–19). Its large rooms are richly furnished and have floor-to-ceiling windows with great views. ✪ Map N2 • Ulitsa Neglinnaya 4 • (495) 783 1234 • Metro: Teatralnaya • www.moscow.park.hyatt.com • €€€€€

General Index

Acknowledgements

The Author
Matt Willis is a widely published travel writer and journalist who has lived and worked in Russia and Eastern Europe for the past decade.

Photographer
Demetrio Carrasco

Additional Photography
Rough Guides/Jonathan Smith

Fact Checker
Marc Bennetts

Maps
JP Map Graphics

FOR DORLING KINDERSLEY

Publisher
Douglas Amrine

List Manager
Christine Stroyan

Design Manager
Sunita Gahir

Senior Editor
Sadie Smith

Project Editor
Alexandra Farrell

Senior Cartographic Editor
Casper Morris

Cartographer Stuart James

DTP Designer Jason Little

Production Controller
Sophie Argyris

Picture Credits

t-top, tl-top left; tlc-top left centre; tc-top centre; tr-top right; cla-centre left above; ca-centre above; cra-centre right above; cl-centre left; c-centre; cr-centre right; clb-centre left below; cb-centre below; crb-centre right below; bl-bottom left, b-bottom; bc-bottom centre; bcl-bottom centre left; br-bottom right; d-detail.

Aleksandr Sergevich Pushkin with his wife, Natalya Goncharova, at the Court Ball, 1937 (oil on canvas), Nikolai Pavlovich Ulyanov (1875–1949) 42cl.

Courtesy of COMRADE HOSTEL: 112tr

CORBIS: Kuror Alexander 30-31; Arcaid/David Clapp 35tl; Dean Conger 48tl, 82cr; Franz Marc Frei 88cr; Grand Toor 24-25c; ITAR-TASS/Lystseva Marina 48c; Georges de Keerle 18-19c; Olivier Martel 13bc; Velikzhanin Victor 15bc.

EYE UBIQUITOUS: Stephen Rafferty 32bl.

JOHN FREEMAN: 62cr.

Courtesy of HM HOSTEL: 112tc.

Courtesy of KITA INN BED AND BREAKFAST: 113tr.

LEONARDO MEDIABANK: 58tl.

PHOTOLIBRARY: age fotostock/Woitek Buss 42bc; age fotostock/Tom Cockrem 12-13c; Ganzalo Azumendi 12br; Tibor Bognar 13tc; Rob Crandall 32tl; Lebrecht Music & Arts Photo Library 42tr, 43tl; Christopher Rennie 100-101; Ellen Rooney 48bl; Liba Taylor 80-81; David Toase 8c.

GREGOR M SCHMID: 14bc.

Courtesy of SPUTNIK HOTEL: 114tc.

TOPFOTO.CO.UK: RIA Novosti 33tl.

Courtesy of UNCLE PASHA: 113tl.

VISAGE MEDIA SERVICES: Epsilon 48tr, 49tl; John Freeman 40bl, 60-61; Simeone Huber 62t.

Courtesy of ZOLOTOI KOLOS HOTEL: 114tr.

Phrase Book

In this guide the Russian language has been transliterated into Roman script. All street and place names, and the names of most people, are transliterated according to this system. For some names, where a well-known English form exists, this has been used – hence, Leo (not Lev) Tolstoy. In particular, the names of Russian rulers, such as Peter the Great, are given in their anglicized forms. Throughout the book, transliterated names can be taken as an accurate guide to pronunciation. The Phrase Book also gives a phonetic guide to the pronunciation of words and phrases.

Guidelines for Pronunciation

The Cyrillic alphabet has 33 letters, of which only five (а, к, м, о, т) correspond exactly to their counterparts in English. Russian has two pronunciations (hard and soft) of each of its vowels, and several consonants without an equivalent. The right-hand column of the alphabet, below, demonstrates how Cyrillic letters are pronounced by comparing them to sounds in English words. However, some letters vary in how they are pronounced according to their position in a word. Important exceptions are also noted below. On the following pages, the English is given in the left-hand column, with the Russian and its trans-literation in the middle column. But in the Menu Decoder section the Russian is given in the left-hand column and the English translation in the right-hand column, for ease of use. Because there are genders in Russian, in a few cases both genders and feminine forms of a phrase are given.

THE CYRILLIC ALPHABET

А а	**a**	**a**limony
Б б	**b**	**b**ed
В в	**v**	**v**et
Г г	**g**	**g**et (see note 1)
Д д	**d**	**d**ebt
Е е	**e**	**ye**t (see note 2)
Ё ё	**e**	**yo**nder
Ж ж	**zh**	lei**s**ure (but a little harder)
З з	**z**	**z**ither
И и	**i**	s**ee**
Й й	**y**	bo**y** (see note 3)
К к	**k**	**k**ing
Л л	**l**	**l**oot
М м	**m**	**m**atch
Н н	**n**	**n**ever
О о	**o**	r**o**b (see note 4)
П п	**p**	**p**ea
Р р	**r**	**r**at (rolling, as in Italian)
С с	**s**	**s**top
Т т	**t**	**t**offee
У у	**u**	b**oo**t
Ф ф	**f**	**f**ellow
Х х	**kh**	**kh** (like loch)
Ц ц	**ts**	le**ts**
Ч ч	**ch**	**ch**air
Ш ш	**sh**	**sh**ove
Щ щ	**shch**	fre**sh sh**eet (with a slight roll)
ъ		hard sign (no sound, but **s**ee note 5)
Ы ы	**y**	l**i**d
ь		soft sign (no sound, but see note 5)
Э э	**e**	**e**gg
Ю ю	**yu**	**you**th
Я я	**ya**	**ya**k

Notes

1) Г Pronounced as v in endings -ого and -его.
2) Е Always pronounced ye at the beginning of a word, but in the middle of a word sometimes less distinctly (more like e).
3) Й This letter has no distinct sound of its own. It usually lengthens the preceding vowel.
4) О When not stressed it is pronounced like a in **a**cross.
5) ъ, ь The hard sign (ъ) is rare and indicates a very brief pause before the next letter. The soft sign (ь, marked in the pronunciation guide as ') softens the preceeding consonant and adds a slight y sound: for instance, n' would sound like ny in 'ca**ny**on'.

In an Emergency

Help!	Помогите! Pomogite!	pama**geet**-ye!
Stop!	Стоп! Stop!	stop!
Call a doctor!	Позовите врача! Pozovite vracha!	paza**veet**-ye **vra**cha!
Call an ambulance!	Вызовите скорую помощь! Vyzovite skoruyu pomoshch!	**vi**zaveet-ye **sko**ru-yu **po**mash'!
Fire!	Пожар! Pozhar!	pa**zhar**!
Police!	Милиция! Militsiya!	meel**eet**see-ya!
Where is the nearest...	Где ближайший... Gde blizhayshiy...	gdye bleez**hay**sheey...
...telephone?	...телефон? ...telefon?	...tyelye**fon**?
...hospital?	...больница? ...bolnitsa?	...bal'**neet**sa?
...police station?	...отделение милиции? ...otdelenie militsii?	...atdyel**yen**ye meel**eet**see-ee?

Communication Essentials

Yes	Да Da	da
No	Нет Net	nyet
Please	Пожалуйста Pozhaluysta	pa**zhal**sta
Thank you	Спасибо Spasibo	spas**ee**ba
Hello	Здравствуйте Zdravstvuyte	zdr**a**stvooyt-ye
Goodbye	До свидания Do svidaniya	da sveed**a**nya
What?	Что? Chto?	shto?
Where?	Где? Gde?	gdye?
When?	Когда? Kogda?	kagd**a**?

Phrase Book

Useful Phrases

How are you?	Как Вы Поживаете?	kak vee pozhivaete?
	Kak vee pozhivaete?	
Very well, thank you	Хорошо, спасибо	kharasho, spaseeba
	Khorosho, spasibo	
How do I get to…?	Как добраться до…?	kak dabrat'sya da…?
	Kak dobratsya do…?	
Do you speak English?	Вы говорите по-английски?	vi gavareet-ye po-angleeskee?
	Vy govorite po-angliyski?	

Eating Out

A table for two, please	Стол на двоих, пожалуйста	stol na dva-eekh, pazhalsta
	Stol na dvoikh, pozhaluysta	
The bill, please	Счёт, пожалуйста	shyot, pazhalsta
	Schet, pozhaluysta	
breakfast	завтрак	zaftrak
	zavtrak	
lunch	обед	abyet
	obed	
dinner	ужин	oozheen
	uzhin	
waiter!	официант!	afeetsee-ant!
	ofitsiant!	
waitress!	официантка!	afeetsee-antka!
	ofitsiantka!	
dish of the day	фирменное блюдо	feermenoye blyooda
	firmennoe blyudo	
appetizers; starters	закуски	zakooskee
	zakuski	
main course	второе блюдо	ftaroye blyooda
	vtoroe blyudo	

Menu Decoder

белое вино	byelaye veeno	white wine
beloe vino		
вода	vada	water
voda		
жареный	zharyenee	roasted/grilled/fried
zharenyy		
икра	eekra	black caviar
ikra		
икра красная/ кета	eekra krasna-ya/ kyeta	red caviar
ikra krasnaya/ keta		
красное вино	krasnoye veeno	red wine
krasnoe vino		
курица	kooreetsa	chicken
kuritsa		
мясо	myasa	meat
myaso		
печёнка	pyechyonka	liver
pechenka		
печёный	pyechyonee	baked
pechenyy		
пиво	peeva	beer
pivo		
морепродукты	moryeprodooktee	seafood
moryeproduktee		
сыр	sir	cheese
syr		
сырой	siroy	raw
syroy		
яйцо	yaytso	egg
yaytso		

Staying in a Hotel

Do you have a vacant room?	У вас есть свободный номер?	oo vas yest' svabodnee nomyer?
	U vas yest svobodnyy nomyer?	
single room	одноместный номер	adnamyestnee nomyer
	odnomestnyy nomer	
double room with double bed	номер с двуспальной кроватью	nomyer s dvoospal'noy kravat'-yoo
	nomer s dvuspalnoy krovatyu	
key	ключ	klyooch
	klyuch	

Time

one minute	одна минута	adna meenoota
	odna minuta	
one hour	час	chas
	chas	
Monday	понедельник	panyedyel'neek
	ponedelnik	
Tuesday	вторник	ftorneek
	vtornik	
Wednesday	среда	sryeda
	sreda	
Thursday	четверг	chyetvyerk
	chetverg	
Friday	пятница	pyatneetsa
	pyatnitsa	
Saturday	суббота	soobota
	subbota	
Sunday	воскресенье	vaskryesyen'ye
	voskresene	

Numbers

1	один/одна/одно	adeen/adna/ adno
	odin/odna/odno	
2	два/две	dva/dvye
	dva/dve	
3	три	tree
	tri	
4	четыре	chyetir-ye
	chetyre	
5	пять	pyat'
	pyat	
6	шесть	shest'
	shest	
7	семь	syem'
	sem	
8	восемь	vosyem'
	vosem	
9	девять	dyevyat'
	devyat	
10	десять	dyesyat'
	desyat	
11	одиннадцать	adeenatsat'
	odinnadtsat	
12	двенадцать	dvyenatsat'
	dvenadtsat	
20	двадцать	dvatsat'
	dvadtsat	
100	сто	sto
	sto	
1,000	тысяча	tisyacha
	tysyacha	
2,000	две тысячи	dvye tisyachi
	dve tysyachi	
5,000	пять тысяч	pyat' tisyach
	pyat tysyach	

Selected Street Index

Key to abbreviations
Ul. *Ulitsa* **Pl.** *Ploshchad* **nab.** *naberezhnaya* **per.** *pereulok*